MW01690302

The Lourdes *of* Psychotherapy

Originally published as

The Lourdes of Arizona

Spanish language version:
El Lourdes de Arizona,
translated by Renato Valenzuela and
published by Cuatro Vientos, Santiago, Chile

Efforts to compare what happened in Arizona to what happened in the Second Vatican Council or Woodstock — though still unscientific — should not be altogether repudiated. It is becoming increasingly important to prove you were there in order to persuade graduate students and even some department heads of your commitment to the learning process, of your wish to help clients, and of your association with big-shots and miracle workers in this century's field of therapy. Any relics you may have in your possession such as a program or a picture or a receipt for a non-refundable deposit are likely to increase in value. Hold on to them. There's no need to get them carbon-dated.

— Braulio Montalvo
Family Therapist

The Lourdes *of* Psychotherapy

by Carlos Amantea

Milton H Erickson
Foundation Press

2005

Phoenix, Arizona

First edition
Copyright © 1989
Lorenzo W. Milam

First edition, Second printing
Copyright © 2005
Milton H. Erickson Foundation

All rights reserved.
No part of this book may be reproduced by any process whatsoever without the written permission of the copyright owner.

Published by
The Milton H. Erickson Foundation
3606 North 24th Street
Phoenix, AZ 85016
www.erickson-foundation.org

The Lourdes of Arizona appeared in *The Fessenden Review,* Vol. XI, Nos. 1, 2, and 3 in slightly different form (subscription address: Box 7272, San Diego, CA 92107), Parts of the description of the meeting with Milton Erickson were published in *The Sun* (412 W. Rosemary, Chapel Hill, NC 27514). *The Family Therapy Networker* (7703-13th Street, N.W., Washington, DC 20012) also published excerpts from the final manuscript.

Note: The Milton H. Erickson Foundation expressed reservations and concerns regarding the publication of the R. D. Laing interview. The reservations included the fact that the interview printed as such could lead to significant misunderstandings and misinterpretations.

Library of Congress Cataloging-in-Publication data
Amantea, Carlos A., 1933-

The Lourdes of Arizona.
Includes index.
ISBN: 1-932248-23-4
1. Evolution of Psychotherapy Conference (1985. Phoenix, Ariz.) I. Title.
RC480.5.A48 1989
616.89 ' 14 88-33666

Manufactured in the United States of America
10 9 8 7 6 5 4 3 2

Mrs. Rooney: *I remember once attending a lecture by one of these new mind doctors, I forget what you call them. He spoke . . .*
Mr Rooney: *A lunatic specialist?*
Mrs. Rooney: *No no, just the troubled mind, I was hoping he might shed a little light on my lifelong preoccupation with horses' buttocks.*
Mr. Rooney: *A Neurologist?*
Mrs. Rooney: *No no, just mental distress, the name will come back to me in the night. I remember his telling us the story of a little girl, very strange and unhappy in her ways, and how he treated her unsuccessfully over a period of years and was finally obliged to give up the case. He could find nothing wrong with her, he said. The only thing wrong with her as far as he could see was that she was dying. And she did in fact die, shortly after he washed his hands of her.*
Mr. Rooney: *Well? What is there so wonderful about that?*
Mrs. Rooney: *No, it was just something he said, and the way he said it, that has haunted me ever since. When he had done with the little girl he stood there motionless for some time, quite two minutes I should say, looking down at his table. Then he suddenly raised his head and exclaimed, as if he had had a revelation, 'The trouble with her was she had never really been born!'* [Pause] *He spoke throughout without notes.* [Pause] *I left before the end . . .* [Sobs] *There's nothing to be done for those people!*
Mr. Rooney: *For which is there? . . .*

—*All That Fall*
by Samuel Beckett

about the author

Carlos Amantea has published twelve books and is a critic for RALPH - The Review of the Arts, Literature, Philosophy, and the Humanities at www.ralphmag.org

The author wishes to thank Jeff Zeig of the Milton H. Erickson Foundation for his comments on and corrections to the article as it appeared in *The Fessenden Review* and Dr. Gil Spielberg of San Diego who gave comments on the manuscript. He would also like to thank Cathy Conheim of San Diego who started him on this particular journey.

Carlos Amantea is one of the many pseudonyms of Lorenzo W. Milam.

The Lourdes *of* Psychotherapy

PART I

R. D. Laing

CHAPTER 1

Question (addressed to Dr. Carl Whitaker): You don't know me but I know you.
Whitaker: I don't know me either.

R. D. Laing is a tweedy and pleasant-faced Scot who avoids the lingual tricks of the mind-change trade. With his Scottish accent ('Ego' for example becomes *Egg-o*, as in Eggo Waffles) and with his Oxfordian good looks, he comes across more like a doyen of English literature rather than one of the most controversial practitioners of psychotherapy in England and the United States.

This morning, the first morning of the conference entitled *The Evolution of Psychotherapy,* someone in the Phoenix Convention Center Maintenance Department has turned on all the air conditioners rather than the heaters. It is December 11, 1985, and for the first time in forty years, measurable snow has fallen in Maricopa County. I confide to my seat-mate that Laing had *ordered* the cold air as some sort of obscure psychological test of his audience. "He wants to see who will be the first to react, to complain about the cold, to walk out," I say. Then he will award a therapeutic medal of honor, Authority Defiance of the First Order or some such. Tricks and paradoxes are all the rage in contemporary psychotherapy to test the resistance of the various patients (or "clients," in the preferred lingo of the trade). In any event, with the frigid blasts of cold air, and the absence of light, Laing has our unbounded if shivery attention. I am reminded of lectures in medieval France that took place in dark rooms so that no one could take notes and thereby steal the ideas of the professor.

"All attempts to describe what goes on between me and my patients falls apart when I speak to a group like you," he starts off. "I'll be interested to see what I have to say. In a curious way, I am not myself all the time. I take my ego to be a schema; it is not fully a conscious part of me. It's an auto-illusion. One can lose oneself in the presentation of the self to the self as an ego," he says. "What the hell is he talking about?" I think. "No wonder it's so cold," I think. "This is like the penguins at Sea World." Since they are out of their natural habitat, the habitat is brought to them: ice, cold, icy seawater. "Laing's natural habitat is the freezing Islands of Orkney, so he had them turn on the cold here so that he would feel at home."

"One cannot understand another person without understanding what it is to *be*," he continues. "Love isn't enough. One needs a skillful means to facilitate transformation. One cannot use a technique in order to be oneself. The beginning of therapy is one of scanning the situation to find the easiest, quickest, cheapest, and least painful way in which patient and therapist can gain access to each other."

Laing's schtick has been to dismay the psychiatric profession by his eccentric behavior, strange writings, and unusual psychotherapeutic techniques. He claims that one can never pre-plan a system of 'intervention' (to use the phrase most popular in therapy) but just has to let it happen. And he is not alone in the fraternity in feeling that *feeling* is the key; indeed, he is in good company with, for example, Rollo May, Virginia Satir and others in claiming that there might be elements of some kind of telepathy between therapist and patient. No wonder the traditionalists feel uneasy with the likes of Laing. "People are usually suffering from the past when they come to see us," he says, "and the problem is — how do we move them into the present?" Here, he gets even more daring: "Does it go back to one's youth, one's birth, or one's death in a previous lifetime? Some people feel they have died, and have not been *reconceived*, much less reborn. In this, we have to suspend our disbelief. One does not have to go over the hill or over the wall to let the client be anywhere in that wheel between birth and death, between death and rebirth."

■ ■ ■

The Phoenix Hyatt Regency, the host hotel for the conference, looks like a giant peyote plant on a stick, and the innards have all the charm and grace of Folsom Prison. From the three glass-wall elevators in the lobby, you can descend past 500 or 600 cell doors, all decorated with meganumbers for us blind and absent-minded prisoners.

It is the presence of Laing and twenty-five other heavies of the world of psychotherapy that brings people from across the United States and from dozens of other countries to this meeting. Salvador Minuchin, Bruno Bettelheim, Albert Ellis, Paul Watzlawick, Carl Rogers, James Masterson, Jay Haley, Carl Whitaker, Virginia Satir, Murray Bowen, Rollo May: the gurus, the masters, the stars in the diadem of psychology, psychotherapy, social work, counseling and family therapy — many of them brought together for the first time. These names may mean little to those who are not in the "change" profession — but to the *cognoscenti* — they are the wizards. It would not be unlike having a writer's conference with Gabriel Garcia Marquez, Isaac Bashevis Singer, Tom Wolfe, Joan Didion, Yevgeny Yevtushenko, Jerzy Kozinski, and John Barth — all under one roof. Or it would be like having an all-star baseball conference with Ted Williams, Dave Murphy, Joe DiMaggio, Micky Mantle, Dave Winfield, Orel Hershiser, and Stan Musial.

In any event, Laing, Bettelheim, et al. are gathered in Phoenix for the better part of the week. And a conference which was designed for 2,000 people has blossomed into one with 7,200 attendees, with another 3,000 to 4,000 turned away. As the originator of the conference, one Jeff Zeig, said, "It's the Woodstock of Psychotherapy."

Zeig is a therapist in his own right, and a young disciple of the late eccentric Milton Erickson. All agree that it was a miracle that he had gotten so many of the top-drawer savants to join in on this venture. The second miracle is that they were willing to appear on the same panels with others, often bitter professional enemies, some even considered to be authentic crackpots. Salvador Minuchin, one of the mavens of Family Therapy, suspected to be rather quirky himself, at one point refers to his fellows here as "psychiatrists, psychologists, Zulus, and Eskimos."

■ ■ ■

Carl Whitaker and his sidekick David Keith call themselves "genuine imitation psychiatrists." Their first presentation is more like that of Chico and Groucho Marx. Whitaker says he decided to take on a cotherapist "because I was so afraid of appearing stupid . . . . I found that I was in the imitation psychiatry business, and the people in front of me were in the imitation patient business." Whitaker delights in making heavy fun of his profession, not to say those he treats, with such statements as: "Schizophrenia is a disease of abnormal integrity," "Six months after you cure a schizophrenic, they're back with their mother again — crazy as hell again," "Families of schizophrenics are abnormally normal," "We're all crazy. I have delusional visions every night between 11 P.M. and 7 A.M. It's called dreaming."

Whitaker looks not unlike an ageing deliveryman for the north Jersey Schlitz beer route. He is not only an apologist for madness, he encourages it. "It's craziness that gives you courage — that's where life is." His favorite apothegm about schizophrenics is that they are stupid. "You and I may want our mothers to breastfeed us even though we're forty years old, but we don't act on it. The schizophrenic will not only want to be breastfed, he will go down to the street corner downtown and ask the corner policeman to do it, even though," he adds tartly, "the policeman just isn't equipped properly. If you are smart, you just aren't considered to be crazy."

"Look at Picasso," says Whitaker, "he was crazy. There are people in our society who are crazy as hell who make a living. [Pause]. I make a living."

Later, on families: "I think divorce is wonderful, but it's really an 'irrevocable trust,' so divorce is the wrong word."

On hallucinations: "All pathology is a function of what we already are. Hallucinations are already a part of society, so one who is pathological just has 'em in high relief."

On teaching psychotherapy: "Anything that is worth knowing in this field cannot be taught. You're just getting a dilution. You can't understand technique just through what we tell you."

Next to Minuchin, Laing, and Albert Ellis, Keith and Whitaker were the "faculty" at the conference who had a good portion of the audience leaving the room, looking troubled and shaking their heads. Keith told about a middle-aged lady who came to him for treatment. She thought she was being followed by the police.

"Are you working with them?" asked Keith.

"Working with who?" asked the lady, suspiciously.

"The Wisconsin board of psychiatric evaluators," he said. "I read in the newspaper that they are investigating all the therapists in the state, looking for malpractice."

"I don't know what you are talking about," says the lady.

"O come on," said Keith. "I know one when I see one. I'll bet that pin on your chest is really a microphone."

"Are you crazy?" she said. "It's a pin. Touch it. I'll show you."

"O no you don't," said Keith. "Now I *know* you are trying to trap me."

Of course as this goes on, a certain transference takes place, with Keith coming on so much more looney than the patient that, soon enough, she begins to move away from her madness to accommodate him. As Keith describes it, "My being crazy with her flipped her into playing the role of the sane one."

▪ ▪ ▪

In the exhibition hall, amongst all the book stalls, tape

stalls, and real-life-doll stalls, they have the Milton Erickson Memorial Bronze Project. It sports one of those jut-jawed sculptures of him, bright of metallic eye, balanced on a wrought base. It nestles uneasily next to statuary of wild horses in various states of jumping and running, and, for social and political reasons far beyond my ken, a carving of Abraham Lincoln. I wonder what Erickson would have thought of this nonsense, putting his image amongst the broncos and politicos.

It is ostensibly under the sponsorship of the Erickson Foundation that this conference is taking place at all. I think he would have been mildly amused by that too. Erickson was an iconoclast and a maverick, and anything but a conference man. For the fifty or so years of his practice, first in Michigan and later in Arizona, he was one of the most paradoxical of professionals in the mind-change business. An M.D. by training, schooled in traditional psychoanalytical methods — he evolved into a trickster (in the Oriental sense), a hypnotherapist who used a myriad of mind-boggling techniques to convince, jolly, encourage, and coerce his patients into changing.

Erickson is one of the most recorded of psychotherapists. Yet, despite multitudes of sound and video tapes of him in action, there is a swirl of controversy over exactly what he was doing — or thought he was doing. He used, for example, subtle methods of putting people into trances, which, he said, gave him direct access to their subconscious. Once there he could invoke change in habits, feelings, attitudes, fixations, hurts, and general stuckness, using techniques which have been the envy of and mystery to thousands of others in the helping profession, those who were and are attempting to work in the startling muddle called the human mind.

Erickson was a subject of controversy during most of his life, being a psychotherapeutic Peter Pan who was almost always on the cutting, if not actual, edge with his various techniques and elaborate "reframings." Part of the legend was created by Erickson himself. He published a newsletter and a number of books which contained stories of the problems brought to him, how he undertook his various strategies, and some of the requirements he imposed for treatment and remission.

Unlike the usually secretive psychoanalists and psychologists, he regaled students and visitors with stories of patients who were cornered or conned into changing. One of the most famous of these is contained in the book *Uncommon Therapy* by Jay Haley:[1]

Interviewer: To get back to adolescent schizophrenia. Suppose someone called you and said there was a kid, nineteen or twenty years old, who has been a very good boy, but all of a sudden this week he started walking around the neighborhood carrying a large cross. The neighbors are upset and the family's upset, and would you do something about it. How would you think about that as a problem?

Erickson: Well, if the kid came in to see me, the first thing I would do would be to want to examine the cross. And I would want to improve it in a very minor way. As soon as I got the slightest minor change in it, the way would be open for a larger change. And pretty soon I could deal with the advantages of a different cross — he ought to have at least two. He ought to have at least three so he could make a choice each day of which one. It's pretty hard to express a psychotic pattern of behavior over an ever increasing number of crosses.

By telling these long and often very funny stories about

the people who came to him with their problems, along with description of the spells, hallucination inductions, instructions, and mind-boggling mind-adjustments that he slipped to them, Erickson is violating one of the unspoken interdictions of his profession. Not only are patients expected to be given rigorous anonymity — their problems are to be treated anonymously as well. Clinical studies and reports can be presented for edification and instruction to certain restricted groups, for instance, other therapists, or students, but the tales produced thereby are chaste and dour. In contrast, the stories related by Erickson — especially the ones appearing in Haley's book — are often Zen-like in their details, and are set in such a way that they cannot help but amuse and delight the reader.

One of the basic tenets of Erickson's methodology is that the subconscious has a reason all of its own, separate from what we think of as "logic." In its own way, it is just as consistent as the conscious mind. For example, if you are given to migraines, they are there for a very good reason. They serve some extralogical purpose in your life, the exquisite pain fulfills a scarce realized requirement of your subconscious. If a therapist wants to contain them, the medico might, for example, make provision to have the headaches put in an appearance at a specific time, for instance, every Tuesday afternoon, from 3 to 4 P.M., an hour that is convenient for the patient *and* the subconscious.

Thus, much of our "non-specific" pain fulfills a specific purpose — and we must honor that purpose. And if anything speaks to the central theory of Erickson, it is the notion that the subconscious must be, at all times, respected. Valium, pain pills, shock treatment, medications of any kind, most certainly lobotomy and insulin therapy are violative of the elegant processes of the mind, for they brutally attempt to club it into submission, into what *we* think its priorities should be. The role of the therapist, according to Erickson, is to make contact with the part of the psyche that doctors think of as the "involuntary" part — and find out what *its* needs are. At all costs, we are to respect it. It was said that Erickson believed that his own subconscious could be in direct contact with the subconscious of his patients, and through that dual-trance interaction, appropriate patterns of cure, or at least remission, could be instituted.

Rollo May

CHAPTER 2

There are several advantages to being a member of the working press at "The Evolution of Psychotherapy" Conference. One is that we get into any of the lectures, workshops, and demonstrations, no matter how crowded (and several were jammed). Hardworking M.S.W.'s from Bakersfield and New Haven are moved over to make room for us. Another is that we were not required to ante up the hefty $250 registration fee. (Someone multiplied the fees times the number of participants and figured out the gross at slightly under $1,800,000 for the five day conference.) A third is that we get the comforts and luxuries of a twentieth century press room on the second floor of the South Convention Complex. Finally, we get the chance to attend the once-a-day press conferences, held there at 1 P.M.

Whoever devised the pairings was certainly of a waggish persuasion. We have truck-driver Carl Whitaker at the same time as the urbane R. D. Laing. Virginia Satir[2] was at the table with the authoritative Bruno Bettelheim. Carl Rogers appeared on his own, but later in the day, the respectable Judd Marmor of UCLA turned up in the same session as raucous Albert Ellis.

Of all the participants, only Bettelheim reminded us of the "traditional" shrink of our earlier fantasies. He was courtly, scholarly, and earnest — a man who spoke with the integrity and insight of a half century of practice, of immense concern with humanity's direction and the nature of evil (he spent two years in a Nazi concentration camp).

Dr. Marmor, on the other hand, looked more like your typical Beverly Hills psychiatrist, "Shrink to the stars" (as it were). Bald, tan, short, and stolid, he was unwilling to put his foot anywhere but firmly on the ground, certainly not in his mouth. In apposition, he was paired with Albert Ellis, Ph.D. Albert Ellis, oy!

Albert Ellis might well have been a New York taxi driver in another life, or — for all I know — might still be one. He tends to talk on at length, with the wild song of the Bronx in his voice. One might safely say that his responses to our reportorial questions were speeches, and these speeches as studies in circularity. "Well, you might say that I pioneered sexuality studies in the United States," he would say, "and what we did was to point out that the orgasm, to be effective, has to be studied, not as thoroughly as you know, Masters and Johnson, but in our studies, we found that it could be a matter of fetishes, you know, we have fetishes in our society, and in one of the letters I wrote to the *New York Times*, I said that they were not getting to the heart of the matter [he pronounces it 'hot']. It was a fetish, you know what a fetish is — like in your primitive societies, as we show in Rational-Emotive Therapy, which I pioneered, you can understand what most people mean by your masturbation, your anal sex, your coitus," etc, etc. Dr. Marmor was covertly looking at his watch, and I was wondering how one who pioneered in sexology could possibly pronounce the word "coitus" like a local stop on the IRT-Carnarsie line.[3]

At one point a reporter from the *Kansas City Star*, a blowsy sort with large gut and a nose right out of J. P. Morgan, a reporter who apparently had come to the conference through some delicious timewarp, asked Ellis and Marmor if they believed in Liberal Sex. He handled the two words with the same care that one might use in displaying a dead but an especially large rat, and as Dr. Marmor was politely trying to rephrase ("I am not so sure what you mean by 'liberal sex,'") Ellis jumped in with all *lapsus linguae* intact, eyebrows leaping, arms waving, giving *his* definition of sex, which wasn't necessarily liberal and most certainly wasn't comprehensible, being of the Walter Wandervogel school of sex-definitions, at least so it seemed to me. His extended exegesis and the late hour moved me to steal out the press room door.

■ ■ ■

Meanwhile, back at the Hall of Shivers, Laing is discussing a woman who had come to him because she was "beginning to feel a compelling longing or need not to move." The case had been discussed by him in his recent autobiography:[4]

> *If she became motionless, she could just about get herself moving again with great effort. Morever, she felt an equally compelling pull within her to say nothing. In other words she was moving into catatonic-mutism for, as usual, no ascertainable reason.*

Laing confesses that he had no idea what to do for the lady, and for some of the hour, they merely sat looking at each other. She was very frightened, not of him, but of what might be happening to her. The worst fear of the Western World: *I'm out of control. I cannot control myself. What am I going to do?* One day, for example, around nine or so, she had been raising a cup of tea to her mouth, and she dropped into being motionless, and sat there, frozen, until 4:30 or so in the afternoon.

"The usual diagnosis," according to Laing, "would be catatonia with mutism, with absence of delusional content, and most doctors would immediately commit her to a mental hospital, electric shocks to get her moving again." Mental hospitals are not Laing's style.

"*What do you do when you don't know what to do?*" he asks. "We sat there for the better part of an hour. I don't know why — she either couldn't or wouldn't speak. But what I felt was that we went into a suspended time space, shared, and said nothing. I told her she could come back. She was very aware of the fact that if she fell into someone's hands who would put her in a hospital — she was very aware of what they would do to her."

He continues the tale in his book:

> *She came back three months later . . . . She had got herself a job as a model in an art school. There she remained motionless and speechless for hours on end, and got paid for it. She had the brilliant intuition to market her catatonia. Her job was perfect therapy. She did not mind what position she was put in, as long as she could stay in it for a sizable length of time.*

"It was suggested to me that the best strategy might not always be to try to stop the behavior that is regarded as pathological," he concluded.

Laing in speech is not unlike a Scottish Garrison Keillor. He will halt in the middle of a sentence, apparently grasping for words, and you think "He's not going to make it. He's not going to be able to finish the thought." And you lean forward, awkward, sympathetic, empathetic, and then he breaks through, and goes on to finish the thought brilliantly, then moves to the next idea, in which he again stops, inchoate, apparently wandering, then goes hesitantly on. It drives some people crazy; others find it such an effective technique that they leave feeling wrung out, weary.

Laing, like many of the people at the conference, quoted endlessly from the great epistemologist Gregory Bateson: "He got on with some very peculiar, frightened people, and he said 'I was very unusual because I wasn't frightened of other people's fears.' For better or worse, I'm like that. It's not something I cultivated. I just don't have to be in a state because other people are in a state. There are some patients who I *am* frightened of, and I can't take them on. An Olympic weight lifter who was afraid of his temper came to me, and I said 'I have a friend down the street who's a very good therapist.'"

Like many of his colleagues, Laing spoke to fear, for, after all, what is it that motivates one to seek out "professional help" if it isn't fear? fear of losing one's family, fear of losing one's mind. But Laing claims that the most prevalent fear prevailing today "doesn't have a name. Fear of death, castration: we know all these — as well as claustrophobia, impulse, desire, fear of self."

"But I think the greatest fear, the greatest fear we can identify, which *doesn't* have a name, is . . ." and he pauses, and he pauses too long, and we lean forward, and we shiver, and think "Is he going to be able to finish the sentence? Is he going to leave us with this Truth Half-Formed? Suppose he doesn't complete the thought — we'll never know what is the greatest fear we have today." He puts his head down, grasping for the idea, his face contorted a bit, pulling it out of himself, pulling it out, and then: "The greatest fear for human beings is . . . human beings," and we think "Whew! We got it!"

And then we think "What the hell is he talking about?" He says, "Adults are afraid of children, children are afraid of adults, men afraid of women (with good reason), women afraid of men (for better reason). And how do I deal with it as a therapist? I go for the 'chink of light.' I don't explore the darkness. You have to use your intuition. Your ego has no intuition. That is the point of meditation, and a good deal of my therapy is interpersonal meditation . . . meditating together with the patient."

"Being the mind reader of another person is not being with that person," he says. "And they may think we can read minds, but we can't." Like a good poet, Laing will play with words. One would have to see it written out to realize that here, when he begins to speak of "At-one-ment," he's doing it with and without hyphens at the same time. And when he speaks of him and his patients being "conspirators," he is playing on the Latin *spirare* — to breathe. He is using the Ericksonian technique of breathing in and out with his patients, creating unconscious psychological rapport with them. In Freud's dream work, in his theories of the unconscious, he spoke of the importance of puns and double meanings. Laing utilizes these, and as an example, gives a reading from his book *Knots*:[5]

if it's mine it's not mine
if it's not mine it's mine
if it's mine is not me
if not me is not mine
if not mine
is me

if me is not mine
if not mine is not me
then, if not me, it is me
if not me, it is me
if it is me, it is not mine
if it is not mine it is not me
if it is not me, it is me

if it is me
it is not mine
if it is not mine
it is me
if it is me, it is mine
if it is mine
it is not me
therefore if it is not me
it is mine
if it is mine it is mine

"It's totally mad, isn't it?" he says in conclusion — but to show how effectively he is punning — as he was reading, I was writing as fast as possible, trying to keep up with him, writing his words in case I didn't have the chance to consult the book later, and I wrote "If it's mind it's not me, if it's me it's not mind, if it's not me it's mind, if it's mind then it's not me . . . " *und so weiter.*

It is almost time to quit, but Laing wants to finish up with the tale of the Incubatorium. He starts by telling us a bit about himself: "The most taxing thing for me is my own state of mind. (Sirens go by in the street outside.) I've had to engage in quite a lot of meditation, the in-and-out breathing which was said to be *the* most important form, according to Buddha.

"In ancient Greek medicine, people in psychological

pain would go to the temple, would be ordered to stay down in the basement with the snakes and the mice for seventy-two hours. The priest would tell them, 'You'll be visited by a god or a goddess of the temple. They'll give you a message to give to me.' What they were doing," he says, "was to suspend the active active. By being silent and alone in the Incubatorium, they would stop the thinking mind and have access to the intuitive response — to intuit." He pauses. "It seems to be very shy, this intuitive part of ourselves. Any cynicism, any putting down, makes it run away. And yet, our intuition is where so many of the answers lie."

■ ■ ■

The first night of the conference, my co-worker Ruth and I run into Bruno Bettelheim waiting for the elevator at the Hyatt. "Dr. Bettelheim!" she says. "I've always wanted to meet you. How are you?" He turns away, a bit sullenly, I think, and keeps on punching at the elevator button. Finally, in desperation, he gets in an elevator going down (even though he was punching the UP button).

I tell her not to fret. "I'm sure this happens to him all the time," I say. Still, Bettelheim could learn a few tricks from Milton Erickson. He would always demand a kiss from women who detained him, or asked him a question, or asked for his signature. "Marvelous distancing device," I tell her.

"Bettelheim has to realize that there ain't no such thing as a free lunch," I say, quoting from one of my favorite Social Work teachers. "If he's going to get himself famous, he's going to have to tolerate a little adulation from the likes of us. If he doesn't want groupies," I go on, when we get to the room, "he should start wearing a mask. I'd be happy to get him a mask of me."

"It's not like I was chasing him around," she snaps.

"It's just a little transference. It'll pass," I say.

Ruth and I have worked around each other in our respective trades with sufficient amiability for ten years, but at this point in the conference, for some reason, we are getting tart with each other. Normal people would just tell each other to shut the hell up, but because she and I are so much a part of this Modern Neo-psychology Movement, we have to communicate with each other in more subtle ways.

"The more I know you, the more you seem to me to be borderline," she says, looking out the hotel window.

"My, my — we are getting hostile tonight, aren't we?"

"Borderline, with just a little passive-aggressive," she says. "Where in hell is all this coming from?" I wonder to myself. She's obviously confusing me with her father. He ignores her the first twenty years of her life, and *I* get the blame.

She looks out into the brightly lit city. Her figure is shadowed by the lights from outside. Through the window, I can see the Convention Center, with its great, dark blocks of striated concrete, randomly tumbled all over each other. What is it they call this school of architecture? Yes: New Brutalism.

"I've known you all these years, and I've never known how repressive you can be," she says. Off in the distance, I can see the dark shapes of the Mariposas, hung off against the horizon.

"I suppose you are going to recommend that I go back into therapy?" I say.

"It wouldn't be such a bad idea," she says. "You really

suppress a hell of a lot of yourself."

"I know you're in anger, but what I can't figure out is whether you are also in denial," I say. "Or depression. Or regression. In any event, you're definitely driving me crazy."

She picks up her things and goes out the door. Way off in the distance, I can see a light fluttering at the edge of the hills. Is it the moon struggling to get born out of the mountains. Or is it a mouse? *Parturient montes, nascetur ridiculus mus.*

"She's just like my mother," I think, after she's gone. They both drive me crazy. I never know what they want. I can never give them what they want. And I'll never escape. Ever.

She doesn't really speak to me until the last day of the conference. Ruth, that is. My mother always speaks to me, even when I'm trying not to speak to her. I can always hear her babbling in my head, telling me — patiently and clearly — what I'm doing wrong. She's always right. It drives me crazy.

It isn't until Ruth and I are sitting next to each other on the airplane going back home that we are able to have a decent conversation again. Goddamn shrinks. They'll drive you crazy every day of the week, and twice on Sundays.

That night, my subconscious provides me with the following dream:

I am flying backwards in a DC-3. A cow is looming (and lowing) over my shoulder. The whole thing is taking place in a B-movie, with lousy color definition, and ratty editing technique. The airplane is a cheap green, and the cow a cheap washed-out red. I wake up feeling the strong need for the counsel of Fritz Perls. He would have sat me down and had me make conversation with the various parts of my dream:

"Why are you here?" I would have asked.

"Moo," the cow would say.

"Are you trying to tell me something?"

"Moo."

Then — Perls being Perls — he would have insisted that I make conversation with the airplane. "Where are we going?" I would have said to it.

"Zoom!" the airplane would have replied.

Bruno Bettelheim

CHAPTER 3

The "Evolution of Psychotherapy" Conference *does* become a dream. Bits and pieces of insights, memories, reflections and echoes come up during the whirl of it. We dip in and out of various panels, video tape showings, lectures, discussions. Bruno Bettelheim, during the second day press conference, turns into a kindly old Swiss burgher. He says the trouble with the Helping Profession is that it has created a cadre of people who think they need outside help, instead of feeling they can solve their own problems: "Nothing binds the family together more than knowing they can solve any problem that arises," he says.

And, speaking on the roots of Freud: "His emphasis was always history — the history of one patient. His training was European, thus very philosophical. In America, you grew up on behaviorism, so your therapy (in contrast to Freud) is very manipulative."

How about the modernists — the Brief Therapists, for instance? "Let the children have their fun. American therapists cheat the patient of having his own insight. *You* have to make the discovery. It is not a deep dark truth; but rather, the knowledge that you — the patient —can have a moment of insight."

■ ■ ■

Mary Goulding is animated (not like some of the zombies at this conference), filled with the ebullience of her trade. She is a neo-Gestaltist who practices what she calls *Redecision Therapy*. "Who has been living inside your head?" she asks. "We have to get rid of the self-destructive self-criticism, like a parent telling a child 'Don't be sane, because if you are, then I'll have to know I'm not.' Children make early decisions and these decisions are quite precise. As one grows up, one has to make sense of their lies. They accept their attributes, but all attributes are straitjackets. People have to change their pasts so they can live in the present." She speaks of the delight, the *fun* of being a therapist. "A good therapist loves the work, and I love the change that comes with being a therapist." She remarks on the 60s: "Remember us in the parades for SNCC, with our *I'm OK, You're OK* balloons. It was the Peter Pan in all of us."

From Goulding, I go over to watch Salvador Minuchin in his introductory speech in the lecture hall. Minuchin looks like one of those South American politicians — a bit jowly, with big black-rimmed glasses that tend to hide the eyes. He would look more in place going down the Paseo de la Revolución, stopping to exchange political lore and dirty jokes with the other compadres who run the lives and fortunes of the peasants of Puerto Ángel.

He looks like that, but rather than dealing with petty graft in Oaxaca, he's running the hottest Family Therapy center in the United States, perhaps in the world. And rather than speak in terms of political gossip or *mordita*, he speaks, in accented English, in an elegant style (which has more to do with literature and poetry) of the chaotic world of Family Therapy, and social services, and *change*.

"Remember that thirty years ago, the emphasis was on the patient's internalized pathology. In a mental hospital for children, the parents were visitors, were not part of the treatment. They were considered to be destructive to the environment. In Bettelheim's words, we were looking for a 'parentectomy for life.' Now, in family therapy, we see pathology as a function of the lack of power of the children, and we have to intervene with the whole family to parcel out that power.

"For instance," he says, "anorexia is the way for a girl to take some power over the only thing she can really own, her body. As always, the symptom is merely a byproduct of the problem. Family systems involve alliances and negotiated control. They have agendas, subsystems, and — most of all — power in their dynamics."

From Minuchin I pass on to an address by Rollo May (looking like an ageing but elegant Lincolnesque attorney). His discipline is something called Existential Therapy. "We are all in the process of making myth and understanding myth. Myth is the source of all of our memories, and these myths are much more real than reality. People go to therapists when their myths have broken down, and should leave with new available myths that work. How you think, the experience of self: These are all myths.

"People have a strange idea of evil as being demonic," he says. "But evil is a very necessary thing. Lamblike innocence is not very effective: look at Billy Budd. Anger gives energy and force; the demonic is a source of creativity." He quotes from Abraham Maslow, who defines the first innocence as "what we have as children; and the second innocence is one that is without assumptions. There is no god without a devil, but the manipulative invites violence. Good needs evil," May concludes. "As Nietzsche said, 'The idea of suicide has saved many lives.'"

As I listen to him, I think about those who say that Americans are in trouble because we have no shamans, no gurus, no mystics, no philosophers, no witch doctors, no prophets. Bosh. They are here in Phoenix (appropriate name!). There are twenty-six wizards. They can see, we think, into the hearts and souls of humans, and act on what they see. They act for change, for an end of violence imposed by patients on others, or on the self. We believe that they have magic: Milton Erickson could put a roomful of people into a trance. Jeff Zeig has put a roomful of therapists into the same state at this very conference.

These shamans — they might be the salvation of the country. We have invested these gods and goddesses with great powers (the legal system grants special protections for those in the Mind Profession). At the same time, we have no room for the Eastern gurus, the Rajneeshes. Indeed, we must chase them from our shores. We have our indigenous sacred masters, and they are called psychotherapists. We have no need of swamis from Poona. The shamans are already in place, on Park Avenue, in their ashrams on Lake Michigan, in teak-lined therapy rooms in Beverly Hills, and La Jolla, and Palm Beach, and in Cambridge, the campuses of Georgetown, Santa Barbara, Austin, the consulting rooms of Mt. Sinai, Langham, St. Vincents. We scorn Muktananda, but we do so because he is redundant. His spirit already practices in the Philadelphia Child Guidance Center, or the Georgetown Family Center, or Institute for Study of Psychotherapy, or at the

Center for Humanistic Studies.

It was Muktananda who said, by the way, that therapists have to be wary of infection from their patients: "A healer's vibrations are transmitted into a patient, and a patient's vibrations are transmitted into a healer. As you work with a patient for a long time, his vibrations enter your body, and you are affected by them. As a result, you yourself become a patient." He pointed out that more psychologists and psychiatrists suffer from mental ills than people in any other profession. The therapist "talks to a patient for hours on end, not realizing how much he himself is being affected by the patient's illness."

■ ■ ■

Q. Dr. Laing, in a recent broadcast in England, you shared with Anthony Clair and your audience that you've been deeply depressed for a long time. Now a lay audience listening to you would say: "Well, is this how you want to be? Don't you want to do anything about this? Is this inevitable? Can anything be done?"

Laing. I haven't *enjoyed* being depressed, it's not at all enjoyable, it's miserable. It's just another way of saying I haven't been happy, and not buoyant in terms of not being happy, either. I think there are a lot of people that think that a psychiatrist or a psychotherapist shouldn't be depressed. Actually, psychiatrists have got, I think, the largest suicide rate of any professional group in society.

Whitaker. That's not true. The dentists have outdone us. It's just recent, though.

Q. Well, naturally, if you're depressed, you go to your therapist, in the hopes of finding help.

Whitaker. Ya, we both tried that. It doesn't work.

Q. How did you get over your own depression?

Q. He hasn't. The world hasn't changed enough.

Laing. Well, I don't know whether it's the world. I haven't been able to work out, adequate to me, the reasons why. I appreciate that I'm a lucky man so far — I've had a very fortunate life compared to many many people. It doesn't take the form of not counting my blessings, and not thanking god for them. And I don't think it's made me cynical or embittered, but there it is. I'm sometimes reminded of the old story about Grok who went to see a psychiatrist because he was depressed — you know the "great cloud." And the psychiatrist says, "I don't think I could do anything for you, but what I would recommend is that you ought to go and see Grok." And I *am* Grok, right? I can also say, not to destroy my market entirely, that the fact that *I'm* depressed doesn't seem to deter my patients from getting better, or happier . . .

Q. If I may ask Dr. Whitaker — this morning, Dr. Minuchin said about you, after a number of complimentary remarks, that "there is a certain rigid demand he has that we should accept the truth of our own deaths and the existence of murderous and incestuous feelings in us all." Do you have any comments?

Whitaker. I agree with it. I don't know what to add to it.

Q. The implication was that in the great body of work that you've done, that as far as he could see, this was the only failing in your theories and practice.

Whitaker. You mean that I shouldn't believe in death?

Q. I don't know. I'm really just . . .

Whitaker. That would be intriguing. I assume everybody else is going to die except me. God wouldn't let *me* die because he knows how important I am.

Laing. Don't you realize that death is perfectly safe?

Whitaker. The final orgasm. Ya.

Q. But I think he was also talking about the fact that you see murderous and incestuous feelings in everyone.

Whitaker. Well, I see it in me, and I assume that everyone else is made from the same clay. I assume that I'm insane in the middle of the night when I'm sleeping and having insane dreams and that I'm probably going to die in spite of my wishes to the contrary. And I assume that my incestuous feelings are part of loving my mother. She was around first with the most of what it took.

Q. Well, if you see those in yourself and then project them onto the rest of the world, in the terms of your trade, isn't this sort of narcissistic?

Whitaker. I hope so. If I don't love me, how can I love anybody else?

■ ■ ■

The grand old men of the Evolution conference are Bettelheim, Murray Bowen, and Carl Rogers. Bettelheim is majestic and knowing, Bowen is knowing and very old, and Rogers is absolutely seductive, even as he develops the 'Dowager's Hump.' "It's from leaning forward so earnestly, listening to too many problems of too many troubled people," I think. When Rogers appears in the now warm Ballroom, he gets a standing ovation, of the kind accorded to living legends of which fraternity he most certainly belongs. He wears a string tie, a benign and earnest expression. He's also bald as a hoot owl, and shows much vigor for one so far along in age. Talking to him now would be not unlike having a garrulous but totally sympathetic old uncle to listen to your problems. He smiles fetchingly at the applause, and says "I was really touched by that." He then adds, "It's always best to have it beforehand, anyway."

"After the 40s and 50s — they thought I died in academia," he says, "But I am still here, still working with individuals, doing client-centered interviews." He was one of the first to react to the stultifying nature of psychoanalysis. Rogers, and Fritz Perls, and Adler, and Sullivan, and Satir began trying something not so trying as seven years on the couch. They changed the language to go along with their change in technique. Just as some people are Platonists, and others Aristotelians, some therapists of that age were Freudians, and some — well, something else. The former tended to be more stolid, addicted to 'deep' treatment, more interested in insight than change. The latter modified not only the style but the language of intervention. We didn't do treatment, but interviews. We didn't treat patients; we worked with clients. We didn't cure; rather we facilitated change. It was revolutionary stuff.

The client-centered treatment of Carl Rogers — following the lead of the Jungians, Harry Stack Sullivan and Alfred Adler — could be done once a week, twice a week if there were a crisis. The cost of this could be borne by any middle-class family, and the once weekly appointments could be shoved into an evening to accommodate those who actually worked for a living.

The first people I remember who had been or were being analyzed were wealthy widows and divorcees — people who could afford the time, money, and large change implied in deep analysis. Clients in "client-centered therapy," by contrast, were often troubled rather than desperate (or rich) — and the difference between the two was the difference between one who is coping, however badly, and one who is at the edge.

Rogers created this revolutionary change. Part of the ovation was for that. The other was an acknowledgement of the fact that he is now history.

▪ ▪ ▪

Rogers and his helpmeet, one fusty, old, white-haired, Oklahoma granny by the name of Ruth Sanford, spend an hour *an hour* setting up what's to be done. The two of them, and the two thousand of us. They take questions, slowly, carefully, whispering back and forth, asking that the house lights be raised (or lowered), adjusting the microphones, adjusting the chairs, and then — taking a break. "It certainly is nondirective," I think. And about as interesting as watching grandma and grandpa tend the garden, fix supper, watch TV, pull down the shades, lock the doors, prepare for bed. The two of them with their endless details, fussing, fussing, perpetually fussing.

Finally Rogers selects a woman from the audience who is willing to talk (intimately! in front of 2,000 people!) about her life. A thirty-five year old psychologist from the middle west, who sometime in the past lost her twins by miscarriage. It still grieves her. And as she talks, telling of her doubts, her loss of power, her sadness, Rogers takes each of her sentences, and carefully, very carefully, reshapes the thought, with the same words, always the same words, reshaping them like a snowball, or a ball of clay, molding them so carefully, then handing them back to her. "I'm very confused," she says. "It's really a very confusing situation," he rephrases, and hands the problem back to her. "I feel so helpless," she says. "You find yourself left with a feeling of helplessness," he says. A bit of clay, passed back and forth between the two of them, to be reshaped, molded, perhaps made into some sort of monument — one that is growing outside herself, one that she can externalize so that she will be able to look at it and understand, a little bit, what is going on in the mystery space called mind.

"Maybe I made a very grave error, in not planning sooner for them," she says, and in the dark auditorium, 2,000 people watch the artistry of what they came to call Rogerian analysis, and in the back of that breathless mass of people, a baby starts to cry. "I wonder what I lost," she says. "I'm not quite sure — you *lost*?" he says. [Gentle emphasis. Pause.] And you're the type that likes to win." Synonyms and antonyms of her words are returned to her, in a good volley from the kindly, understanding, empathetic universal listener. Truly, is there anyone who can listen as well as Carl Rogers?

"If I don't have a child, something's missing," she says, and her voice begins to crack. "So if you don't have a child, that leaves a terrible gap, a terrible void," he says. Suspense. The room is crowded with her pain, and the shared pain of so many of us. How can 2,000 people stay so silent? She is silent. And in silent empathy, he says nothing.

He is poised, ready, ready for her next word. Waiting, we are kindly waiting. She is dressed in a black sweater, black pants, black shoes (one of the audience, later, would call it "wearing mourning").

She: "The one thing I wanted — I didn't get."

He: "At some level, to yourself, you're a failure." He nods. "And so that brings a sense of failure."

She: "It's so hard. Especially at Christmas, when we go to visit their graves."

He: "The tragedy continues. Going around . . . it can hit you."

She: "Sometimes I think I should do nothing, just see

what comes of it."

He: "I can't control this as much as I am used to controlling things.[6] And I just want to sit back and see what comes of it."

She: "Yes. Just to see what comes of it . . ."

Later, Rogers was to describe his task as that of being a companion in the client's world, so that he or she can be released. "My use of their words," he says, "makes it safe to go forward. What I am doing is to validate the client's experience and feeling. The key is to be present for your client. There are silences — we've gone as long as fifteen minutes saying nothing — but it's a working silence."

"I think of the transcendental nature of therapy," he concludes. "Both the client and the therapist can transcend the experience, very much like a religious experience."

Salvador Minuchin

CHAPTER 4

Going from a Carl Rogers workshop into a Salvador Minuchin workshop is not unlike taking one of those jets from London direct to Calcutta. The careful, controlled, sweet, noninterventionist therapy is replaced by one that is chaotic, direct, sometimes brutal, sometimes harrowing — where there is screaming and name calling, and even more strange and wonderful unspoken arrangements.

Many of the attendees of the conference have come with the specific purpose of watching Minuchin in action. To hear him is to share in the excitement of Family Therapy, which, to some extent, he has redesigned using the bases established by Murray Bowen (with his concept of "three generations"), Carl Whitaker, and "the School of Milano" among others (among many others, as Minuchin explained in his opening remarks).

The three hour workshop on Family Therapy, presented by Minuchin in the Ballroom was one of the most eagerly awaited, and most heavily attended, of the whole conference. "I am glad this is called the Ballroom," said Minuchin, "because I have often thought in terms of dance, and I see my work as dealing with the dance of family and therapists."

His accent is heavy, Latin American. He often speaks with metaphors as rich as any out of Shakespeare. And since much of his work is done with videotape recorders, which he considers to be indispensable for therapy, he is as at ease with electronic equipment as he is with families (and large and eager audiences, for that matter).

"The patient comes to you when they are stuck," he says. "And it is a dance. There is a contract. They pay you, you help them, and give them hope for the possibility of change. All persons, all individuals are underutilized. We have to help the family to move out from its stuckness," he says.

Minuchin talks briefly of his pilgrimage to meet Milton Erickson two days before he died. "He gave people hope," he says. "He gave them hope that they could pull themselves up by their bootstraps. People emphasize Erickson's sense of technique. But he also used humor, wisdom, acceptance, and most of all, hope. The people that you are treating are not worse off than you, they've just lost hope." In his book *Family Kaleidoscope*,[7] he speaks of acknowledging the patient's problems "as real things. Then," he says, "I smiled, and asked for a new look, a different perspective. It's not that I fail to see what other experts see. I simply prefer another framing."

Minuchin often speaks of the dynamic force of the therapist: "You have power as an expert. You have a body of knowledge that gives power to your rhetoric, and your rhetoric has the power to persuade. Therapy educates the patient to the theories of the therapist. The patient comes to you with the knowledge that something is wrong. They say they want to change — but they really want to change without changing. We have to move them beyond that. I have to change their attributes of fear." As I listen to him, I realize that Minuchin is, as much as anything, a semanticist. Of course, he has to be an expert on language because he is dealing with people through both spoken and body language — what he calls the dance. It is no accident that he is trilingual (English, Spanish, Yiddish). And it is no accident that he is so good at communicating. After all, the 3,000 of us, his eager listeners, are here for a treatment as well — treatment of technique, treatment of world view, treatment of our failings as therapists. *Qui custodiet custodies?* Who is going to take care of those who are supposed to be taking care of us?

I want to set his next presentation before you as carefully as possible, since it is one of the most dramatic performances (in the artistic sense) that I have ever witnessed. It combines the best of Fellini and Carl Dreyer and Chaplin. It is a videotape of one session with a Boston family. There's the father, mother, and two daughters Sarah and Maureen. The family is Jewish. The "IP" (identified patient) is the youngest daughter, Sarah, twenty-two years old, with five attempted suicides. There is the older daughter, Maureen, thirty-six years old, who was born with spina bifida. She works in a secretarial job, but is obviously heavily handicapped with speech and walking impairment. The father is a side-of-the-mouth-talking, pissed-off, working class stiff. The mother has bleach-blond hair and a good case of the Martyred Whines.

A standard therapist would work with the suicidal daughter alone. Not Minuchin. He homes in on Maureen: what does she do; what is the extent of disability; is she more handicapped now than twenty years ago; how much does the family have to help her feed, dress, go to bed, get up; who does it? She is an integral part of the system, and her handicap becomes a metaphor for the family handicap — in Minuchin's words — their stuckness, their enmeshment in each other.

"I am different from Carl Whitaker," says Minuchin. "I choose not to work with an exterior cotherapist. I choose my cotherapist from within the family." In this case, it's Sarah. "But I am not a nurturer," he says: "I'll work with her; later, I'll kick her. I will join with their tragedy, but I will later show them that it is sapping them.

"All my movements are props, scaffolding. Above all I am saying to them, 'What are the possibilities for change?' You're making a mess of your life, and Sarah's life. Do you think you can change?"

Minuchin dips into the videotape, starts it, stops it, explains. The father, mother, and Maureen sit closely bunched together — Minuchin between, and Sarah apart, by herself. He chooses to leave them in the position they've selected. It is, he acknowledges later, significant. Both Bowen and Erickson have pointed to the importance of the physical position families choose with relation to each other when they first come in the room; it's as important as what they do with their hands, their legs, their eyes, their words.

Minuchin comments on the then-him in the tape from a year ago; and we watch the Minuchin-now, with us, there on the stage, sometimes magnified on the screen, as he tells us, frankly (would Bettelheim or Masterson or Rogers ever be so disarmingly honest?) "I don't like this father. He's a bullshitter." To them, on screen, he says, "You are fascinating people. So bright. You know it's wrong, yet you keep on doing it." And to Sarah, "You decided to quit, only you took a very strange exit." A bizarre metaphor for her suicide attempts.

"My goal is to challenge them in their structures," he says. "My attitude is detached ('Why do things when you know they are wrong?'), and I say to the wife not, 'Why don't you change?' but, 'How can you change your husband?' That makes her a partner in the change that must come. The family is an organism, the yin-yang. The message is that change is possible. Sarah has had all the responsibility — she is identified as the pain-in-the-neck, but she has taken the role of nurse. Maureen is going to be the most resistive to change: as dependent, she has the most to lose. In what I do, I always assume there is going to be resistance. If there is no resistance, then something's wrong."

Minuchin thinks in terms of the dance, the music, the ballet of the family members, and the therapist. When asked by a member of the audience if he is a manipulator, he says that he is a very finely tuned instrument. "I will take the information that I have gathered and use it to help the family. I will use every nuance that is available to me. The behavior of Sarah is the context of the family. She must have a directed self-change, and this change must come in the change in her attitude towards her father."

Minuchin acknowledges that attempted suicides are the scariest patients a therapist can take on. "My first target," he tells us, "is that the girl has to leave the session *and I want not to be afraid*. Those who have tried suicide as often as Sarah have a certain expertise."

In video, Minuchin gets up, stands before her, and says, "Who gave you responsibility for being therapist for the whole family? It's crazy." "*This is typical Minuchin*," he says to us. "I pay a lot of attention to moving. Many of my metaphors have to do with moving — dance, closeness."

He intervenes directly, by physically standing between Sarah and her father. "Who gave you that responsibility?" he asks her. "When did you start your job?" And we can hear the voice of her father, booming in, "*We never put any burden on Sarah.*" "That's resistance," says Minuchin-now.

"You should notice how Sarah is beginning to use Salvador Minuchin language: she has accepted the responsibility of being my cotherapist. Someone in the family will agree with you, there will always be *someone*. And that makes your job so much easier."

"Have you always been a parent watcher?" he says on video to Sarah, as she tries to look beyond him to her father. And the audience sighs. The perfect Ericksonian double bind. If Sarah says she has been a parent-watcher for a long time, it means that she admits to what is, after all, a key element of the family stuckness, that is, always watching her father for clues, always looking to him for cues when a question is placed to her, always looking to him. If she says I've only been a parent-watcher for a short time, it means that she is *still* copping to having that lock with him. "When you go out with your father," he asks her, "is he a good companion, or is he boring?" The famous double bind again, with a special arrow aimed at the old man.

Enter Maureen with a question about whether it is her fault. What she means is, "Is it spina bifida's fault?" Minuchin elicits the fact that at one time she walked by herself, was independent. Now she is not — despite a doctor's statement that she should be even more so now. Minuchin: "I'm surprised that you are less able to walk now, even with a walker. I know something is wrong with your body, *but is there something wrong with your brain?*" The audience gasps, the family gasps, Maureen gasps. That Minuchin — he'll get on *anyone's* case!

Minuchin (to Sarah): "You've taken on an impossible job and then you decided to quit. I see now why you want to quit, to take an exit from life. It's a ridiculously crazy job!"

Minuchin (to us): "I have created a therapeutic construction to separate Sarah from the family. The family has defined her one way, and I have chosen to redefine, by metaphor, what's happening in the family. I have to provide the family with a rationale for change. There is here a tremendous amount of love, and a tremendous amount of hate. Sarah feels cheated, and the family sees itself in a self-sacrificial loving way. I join with them, and start to move them on a different pathway. And I have to do it with love; they would give increased resistance if I take on the hate."

Minuchin (to them): "You are a fooked-up family because you love each other too much. I think in this family it's very hard to grow up. How can we help Sarah to grow up? Yours is a depressed family. You [Sarah] are quitting, saying 'fook you,' — saying I'll not spend all of my life taking care of you."

Minuchin (to us): "There is a pattern of tremendous proximity between Sarah and her father. I would have a suspicion of incest somewhere down the line, but they don't screw because it would be redundant. They are so close, and it is at the expense of his wife. My strategy is to challenge this system. I do it by what I say, the way I move. But I also note what they say and do, the way they move. I use them for feedback. Sometimes I try to increase the conflict between them to see how they negotiate conflict. In all that I do, I have to think like a pool shark. To sink a ball, you must hit another ball.

"The mother is already distant from Sarah. Sarah is *trying* to distance herself from the father, and suicide is the only method she's discovered so far to do that. But the father told her that if she killed herself, he would kill himself, so she's even denied a successful death. This family is a violin, with only one string, and it's a funeral march."

At one point we watch Minuchin, who has been on the old man's case, pause for a moment, and then ask him (winningly!) for a cigarette. He says, "I have stopped, for a moment, my attacks on the father. I tell him a story about my aunt who used to go to the Yiddish theater and cry through it all 'because she loved it so.' I have joined with them, not only in hidden metaphor, but in being Jewish, and sad."

This sets the stage for the last scene, where Minuchin has asked the mother and father to discuss, for five minutes or so, how they can help change to come about. The camera watches as this discussion starts, and quickly devolves into a battle, with the father in a raised voice saying how hard he tries, how little appreciated he is. The argument of the ages, or at least of thirty-nine years (they've been married thirty-nine years!) The sordid, tedious, mind-numbing, endlessly circular arguments out of the tenement row-house of South Grimy Boston, where the interaction of the two of them has finally led one of the children to contemplate total self-destruction.

The videocamera then pans to Minuchin on the far side of the room, lounging back, talking easily with Sarah, isolated from the battle, filled with their own ease. There is a murmur from the audience. *We* have become enmeshed with this family, and especially with the sweet and troubled Sarah. We have a commitment to change, and we can see her so much more relaxed now, all of us more relaxed now, turned away from her warning parents (their voices raised in eternal battle, sour music in counterpoint), she starting, perhaps, for the first time, on a new road, her new role, neither as nurse nor as caretaker for the family, and, indeed, no longer as the one who must act out so dangerously for the whole system. Their voices continue as strenuous counterpoint to the change that is taking place, a change unbeknownst to them, a change which will help Sarah to exit from their lives in a far less drastic, a far less hurtful, a far more creative way.

Carl Whitaker

CHAPTER 5

Salvador Minuchin to audience of 3,000 therapists:
"How many of you work with welfare families?"
(Approximately 2,000 raise their hands.)
Minuchin, angrily turning away:
"That's not enough."

Q. What do we know now about being with other people, about working in therapy, that we didn't know fifty or a hundred years ago, at the time of the foundations of psychotherapy?

Whitaker. One of the few things I got out of medical school was that you take a body apart and it turns out they're all exactly the same. And I assume that's true for the psyche and for the family. I assume all families are the same.

Laing. I can't think of any fundamental insight into the nature of human beings and relationships between human beings that people have come up with in the last one hundred years that weren't embedded in the records of literature, poetry, and drama. I don't think we've gone beyond Sophocles, Aeschylus, Euripides, Shakespeare,

Tolstoy. I don't think I needed to read the theory of the double bind to know that people are confused by contradictory messages. Tolstoy describes some of that with *exquisite* clarity and precision in *Anna Karenina* for instance, when he takes apart someone's face. Anna Karenina was looking at — what's her lover's name? — and she can see his forehead, his eyes, his cheeks and his lips all beginning to say different things. And she knows the game is going to be up very soon. He couldn't have said it better.[8] I can't think of anything that I've learned from professional [psychological] writing that I haven't found in those writers.

Q. Then why are we here at this conference?

Whitaker. We pay the rent for those people who live in sand castles.

Laing. There has developed a profession, as we know, which has been partly generated by client demand and partly by the marketing of professionals . . . . People want experts to tell them how to live, how to sneeze, and how to wipe your ass, and how to masturbate, how not to masturbate, how to make love, how to get divorced, how to get married, how to be happy, how to bring up your children. And there's a professional response to that sort of thing.

The *Phoenix Gazette* sends in a lady reporter replete with war paint and delicious bodily configurations who, during the press conferences, is given to such o'erreaching questions as, "With the breakup of American families in the eighties, and all the drugs, alcohol, et cetera, the lack of morals, and AIDs, with all the problems of child abuse et cetera and . . . uh . . . all the people on the streets . . . what do you think is the . . . uh . . . future of . . . American family life et cetera in America? Psychologically, that is."

What Laing, Satir, Bettelheim et al. made of these

laocoön queries is a testament to their years of unravelling the words if not the souls of their patients. What the *Gazette* made of these responses turned up in a headline, "Go For What You Want In Life," which loomed like a mastodon above Ms. Delicious' article.

The *Gazette* is also given to what we might call the pick-and-choose style of sensationalism in their writing. During his speech, Minuchin had said he valued Carl Whitaker for what he taught him, but that "here is a certain rigid demand that we should accept the truth of our own deaths, and the existence of murderous and incestuous feelings in us all." In our press conference with Whitaker, I asked him about this, and he tartly responded that he would be foolish if he did not "accept the truth of his own death." The *Gazette*'s answer to Hedda Hopper put the lay community at total ease about the profession of psychotherapy by reporting:

> *Carl Whitaker admits he hallucinates often and confesses to murderous and incestuous feelings from time to time.*

The *Los Angeles Times* was represented by one Ann Japenga, whose byline appeared a week later with an article in the best *Road-&-Track* School of psychological reportage:

> *A hundred years ago an Austrian neurologist named Sigmund Freud peered under the hood of the human soul and found a previously unnamed gizmo he called the unconscious. The part tended to break down, etc. etc. etc.*

Time Magazine weighed in with John Leo who managed to put some of the words of the participants firmly in the wrong mouths. For instance, Minuchin said that the conference was "a ballet." Leo awarded this *mot* to Jeffrey Zeig, the originator of the conference. *Time* also stated that Virginia Satir ("a peppy speaker with murky ideas") was "the top attraction," suggesting that Leo was in catatonia during the presentations of Paul Watzlawick, Carl Whitaker, Aaron Beck, and James Masterson, not to mention Minuchin and Bettelheim, all of whose sessions were packed enough to be uncomfortable, hot, and squashed. *Time,* along with the *New York Times*, dwelled on the obvious — that few of the wizards of psychotherapy can agree with anyone else in the field, much less the world.

What both reporters missed — indeed, what almost all the media missed — was the fact that this was a one-of-a-kind conference, a circus of diverse, brilliant, challenging practitioners, those who were first responsible (and are still responsible) for leading this country out of the self-defeating, expensive, hidebound, inbred, incestuous, upperclass morass which was and is Freudian psychoanalysis. Freud's followers had a stranglehold on this country's psychological thinking, public policy, and orientation for half-a-century. They only came under respectable and honest challenge in the last four decades, and many of the challengers are still alive and are here at this conference.[9]

■ ■ ■

National Public Radio is represented by Margot Adler. As befits a sound reporter, she talks nonstop in an informed, chaotic, and charming style, changing subjects no more nor less often than your typical all-news radio station. Fortunately, our press conferences were not televised, because she was also given to windmilling her arms about when anything was said that caught her fancy, such as the entrenched and brutal antifeminism in the field of therapy, or the punitive nature of the medical profession. Later, during the conference, she jumped the fence, going from reporter to participant in evening discussion with Dieter Baumann, an analyst from Zurich and the grandson of Carl Jung. Sophie Freud, related in some obscure way to *the old original* Freud, got snowed in at Milwaukee, and the ever resourceful Adler — granddaughter of Alfred, it turned out — substituted as tertiary scion of the apostles, and, it was reported, did a credible job, windmills and all.

■ ■ ■

"There is an unseen presence at this conference," I find myself thinking. "It is all those psychotic, neurasthenic, at-risk, schizo, looney-cakes out there that keep these 7,000 helpers in business." Actually, the presence isn't all that unseen. During Rollo May's talk, Tom o' Bedlam appears near the stage, a man of wild eyes and perfervid mien, a perfect metaphor for the bedeviled characters that turn up in the mental repair factories around the country. He is here, I think to myself, to let us know that we are not alone, that we are being watched by what we call the "IP" (Identified Patients). Unfortunately, the conference masters are not given to toleration of fatuous melancholia, so Tom was led away by one of the many gun-toting security guards that infested the convention center.

Later, as I am going from Resistance with Arnold Lazarus to Strategic Therapy with Cloe Madanes (I always read her name as "Cloe Madness"), I run into another wambling, dishevelled, recalcitrant sort who slipped past the guards. "Should they be keeping him in or should they be keeping him out?" I wonder.

These questions were partially answered when Laing sent out the word that for his next presentation, he would be interviewing someone who was "at risk," (the lingo for someone who's not making it in contemporary society.) The Mariposa County Homeless Alternative Psychiatric Services Center, called CHAPS, cast out a dragnet, and brought in Christy.

For the first twenty minutes, Laing interviews her at the back of the stage. The two of them are alone, in a curtained off section, alone except for the several thousand of us peeking in via the video monitor. Our presence remains unacknowledged except for the moment when she says she despairs of "figuring things out." She asks Laing if he has been able to do so.

Laing. What difference does that make?

Christy. Well you've had more time. Have you figured anything out?

Laing. You don't get any wiser when you get older.

That generates an outburst of laughter from the audience, the huge audience that is peering over their shoulders in this most intimate experience, as intimate as — say — making love. "The poor," I think: "They never get any privacy." Their bedrooms are filled with children, their workplaces with hundreds of fellow-workers — and even when they go to the shrink, there are thousands of us looking over their shoulders, hearing their every word, watching their every move.

Christy looks a bit frayed, but shows herself to be well aware of the nature of the conference, her role in it, the way she is viewed by our profession, and the nature of her own tortured head. At one point she says, "I get things turned around. I get opposites confused. When I write I get my letters confused, I get words confused . . . . Either I tend to be paranoid, or they really are after me — I don't know which." Laing responds to this by saying, "You might be after me for all I know."

Later, when he questions her further about what she feels, she says, "I'm just trying to help you guys get some sense into your brains. I don't know if it's worth it though, you know?"

Christy and Laing chat of this and that, sometimes succeeding, sometimes not, in pretending that so many of us are breathlessly there with them. They talk about Christy's parents (her father is a fundamentalist minister back in the middle west), her guru, the Universal Mind, and The Conspiracy:

Laing. What brought you to Phoenix?

Christy. I was trying to escape the conspiracy, and it didn't work.

Laing. What conspiracy?

Christy. Well, if there is one, I suppose you're a conspirator — so you know already. If there isn't I guess I just imagined it.

At all times, Christy seems to be going in and out of her delusions, but she also plays with Laing, using words that would certainly set off alarm bells for professionals: her fear of having her mind read by doctors, her fear of The Conspiracy, and, at one point, her fear of "getting eaten by the gods."

Laing and Christy, both experienced in their way with the workings of a mind (and mind-doctors), use the conference as a metaphor for what's going on inside:

Christy. They're watching us.

Laing. This whole set-up is an enormous conspiracy, and you're right in the heart of the conspiracy just now. If you came to Phoenix to get away from the conspiracy, you haven't done very well.

Christy. What do you mean?

Laing. Well, you're sitting here in this situation.

Christy. You mean the conference is a conspiracy?

Laing. Ya, of course.

When they terminate their twenty-minute exchange, Laing says that he has to return to the podium, and she asks if she can come along, "to see what you say." This wasn't in the script, but Laing, always the maverick, welcomes her with the other panelists. After all, she does have a certain expertise, a place in the operation. Questions from the audience come at her and Laing — and to the heads of the CHAPS program. At one point, Laing suggests to the audience that it would be impossible for him to communicate what went between him and Christy:

> "When one tries to explain one's awareness of that transpersonal field to people who are not aware of it . . . you know how difficult it is to talk about. Don't be too impatient; don't — because you don't understand it, because you are mystified — don't get angry. Something is happening. Something is happening between us in this hall at this very moment. You can't express it in words. There is a conspiracy, there is a divine conspiracy which has brought us together."

A member of the audience stands up to complain that his explanation is obscure, perhaps purposefully so. A dialogue develops between Laing and the man, and is fascinating as insight into one of the core conflicts running through current psychotherapeutic practice. It is a conflict as old, really, as the one that finally split Freud and Jung. It is the one that rages between those who choose to see psychotherapy as a rational science, with scientific parameters, and teachable techniques; and — on the other hand — those who see it as a process which is either instinctual, or, even more bizarre, a mystical transference of thoughts and feelings between client and therapist.

This particular dialogue ends up with Laing shouting at his interlocutor — presumably another therapist — telling him to step down, to let others be heard:

Man. It seems to me that what seems to be happening is that a vacuum has been created. It reminds me of a professor friend of mine who said, "I feel, I feel, I don't know what I feel, but oh how I feel." And what I'm wondering is, that vacuum allows people in the medical profession to bring zombies to us and we have to work with them. And the vacuum doesn't really, give to me, at least, a feeling of understanding, and when you refuse to understand, refuse, it sounds sort of nirvanish. And although I'm not against that, I think that some kind of clearer explanation, clearer understanding should be given, so we know what we're doing. And when you avoid those things, you're breaking down the whole therapeutic process, it would seem to me. Enlightenment does not come just by remaining silent, although that's a nice feeling.

Laing. This young lady sitting beside me is supposed to be an absolute paranoid schizophrenic on medication. She's sitting here just now perfectly *compos mentus*, perfectly clear, facing this most intimidating situation from this stage, not exhibiting any symptoms of schizophrenic disorder. If you knew of any medication that could do that in twenty minutes, from there to here, would you say you wouldn't give that to a patient? You would have to spend the rest of your life being a biochemist to understand what the chemical affects of that sort of thing is suppose to be in the central nervous system. So you don't know anything about this sort of process. Have the humility to admit that, and keep your place! Instead of the arrogance that you seem to have, to think that you . . . because you don't know something that there's something the matter with those people who do. [Applause.]

Man. No, I didn't say that I don't. I have a mind that can understand, I'm sure you do. And I don't think we should call each other names, and say "arrogance." I think there is more arrogance in silence, sometimes, than there is in expressing wisdom, if somebody has it. If there is wisdom give it to us. But don't let us feel as though there's some kind of a mystical communion going on when there isn't. And to call . . . .

Laing. There is. There is, that's the point. There certainly is. But — see — you say when there's some kind of mystical communion going on when there isn't.

Man. Well again it's "I feel" — "I feel."

Laing. Ya, "I feel," "I feel," "I feel" — who's talking about I feel?

Man. "I don't know what I feel, but, oh, how I feel it!"

Laing. Well — I do know! And you don't know! And I'm saying that it is not verbal. And it can't be put into words. And because you can't understand it, obviously, you say "ha, ha, ha, some sort of mystical communion going on."

Man. But there are people who have claimed to see the devil. There are people who have claimed all kinds of things.

Laing. Give someone else a chance at the microphone!

Man. If it bothers you I can quit.

Laing. [Loudly] It bothers me! [Applause].

After some discussion about drugs in the CHAPS program, (whether the clients are being coerced — as is true in so many street programs — into using drugs by the therapists) Christy was held up by one of the doctors as being as good an example as possible of a street person who had been helped by the program, but then Christy interrupts, saying:

"The reason I'm doing better is because I quit putting mental energy into the conspiracy. And creating it, to a certain point. But this guy says that there is one. And I think that's because you [points to Laing] know how to share minds, because he knows how to tap into other people's minds. You know on a subtle level: not by just asking questions. Because everybody reads minds. You guys read minds. I tell ya, everybody does. And if you observe, if you look around, you'll notice it. Thank you. And I would like to say something else while I got this [microphone]. I don't go around like a paranoid schizophrenic all the time. I know how to keep my cool. And I think this guy would be a great psychotherapist, because he does that. [Laughter] Because he knows how to tap into other people's . . . where other people's minds are at. You know — not by just asking questions and trying to figure things out like some . . . "[Nods at one of the CHAPS doctors].

Salvador Minuchin — not himself on the panel — steps forward out of the audience and addresses himself directly to the CHAPS doctor:

"I think you should learn something from Ronald. Because I don't think you did. You see, what we have experienced here is a communion of love. What I was observing, and I felt in trance, I felt in love with this young person, and she was able to elicit from Ronald, and so did he from her — that kind of experience. It was experienced at the level not of the words, but there was an element of joining, that was expressed in their hands, in their legs, they were moving exactly in the same place, and I loved it. And I think it's important

> that you should know that. I am talking to the physician that talks about drugs. Because the drug that existed there is very, very powerful."

This is followed by Bravos from the audience.

Albert Ellis

CHAPTER 6

One of the themes of the conference is, "Who makes the best helper?" The answer according to several of the faculty, was "The least trained person seems to work out best." This is in keeping with the commonly held belief that any distancing experienced between patient and professional is commensurate with the number of academic degrees the therapist has acquired. Jay Haley, the amanuensis of Milton Erickson and a respected therapist in his own right, says that at one point when he was working with Minuchin in Philadelphia, they had the paradoxical problem of training middle-class assistants to work with the poor, or of training the poor to be therapists. They found that both were equally easy to do, but that "the most difficult people to train to be effective therapists were those who had had the most therapy."

Paul Watzlawick is another family therapist, but in contrast to the raucous Philadelphia School, handles his largely middle-class families in San Francisco with a certain gingerliness. "Intervention has to be small — seemingly silly, unimportant, distant from the problem," he says. His interventions, which he calls "prescriptions," must be cheap, not contrary to one's religion, and must minimize resistance by asking for small changes in behavior. He speaks to the "elegance" of treatment in setting up a paradoxical situation which makes resistance impossible. One of his favorite stories has to do with Milton Erickson who had a rebellious patient who couldn't stop tapping her hand. "Erickson would say to her, 'I want you to keep on tapping your hand.'" In the same way, with a woman who claimed she couldn't say 'No,' "I asked her to go around the room and say 'No' to everyone. The elegance is that she is changed if she does, and changed if she doesn't." Watzlawick says that one of his simplest techniques is what he calls the Worst Fantasy. Patients are asked to tell him the most far-out, impossible, looney, spacey, outlandish, ridiculous fantasy that they can imagine. The response is often a key to what is really going on in their lives, something that may not have come up before. "In our therapy," he concludes, "we assume that every failure is ours and every success is theirs. In all that we do or say or prescribe, we avoid negatives. It turns out that in the evolution of English, like all languages, the words 'no,' 'not,' 'nobody,' 'nowhere,' and 'nothing,' were the very last to appear. 'Don't forget to . . .' amounts to a request to forget. 'Don't upchuck in the car' is an open invitation to a child to vomit in the car."

■ ■ ■

Albert Ellis has decided that all worlds revolve about a theory he constructed called RET (some thought it meant Real Estate Investment Trust, but evidently it's Rational-Emotive Therapy). On the second afternoon, in the appropriately named Ballroom, Ellis has his sparse and somewhat mortified audience join in with a "psychological singalong." He calls his ditties "Rational Humorous Songs" (in case we might miss the levity of it all). A typical one, sung to the tune of "Beautiful Dreamer," is

BEAUTIFUL HANGUP

Beautiful hangup, why should we part
When we have shared our whole lives from the start?
Though you still make me look like a jerk,
Living without you would take so much work!

A follow-up is more daringly titled:

MAYBE I'LL MOVE MY ASS

(To the tune of "After the Ball Is Over")

After you make things easy
And you provide the gas;
After you squeeze and please me,
Maybe I'll move my ass!
Make my life nice and breezy,
Fill it with sassafras!

And possibly, if things are easy,
I'll move my ass![10]

■ ■ ■

Thursday night, exactly midway through the conference, on my way back to the hotel, I fall in alongside a white-haired lady who tells me that she is working with prisoners.

"Where do you work?" I say.

"In Mexicali," she says. "We're from Our Lady of Fatima in El Centro. We cross over the border every day to work with the women in prison on the Mexican side of the border."

"How long have you been doing that?"

"Six years."

"Summer and winter."

"Summer and winter," says Sister Angelica.

That has special meaning for people who know the Imperial Valley. Winter means forty to seventy degrees Fahrenheit. Summer, especially July and August, means day-after-day of billowing heat, often 120 degrees. For ten hours a day, weeks in a row, it's Oven City. It's a place where you look on one of those television weather maps, or on the back page of USA Today, and they show those colors: not green, or yellow, or orange; no, it's blood red. That's how hot it is. And Mexican jails have no air conditioning.

"Some people criticize us, say we should be working with the poor over here or over there," she says. "But I think the ones in prison . . . they need help. We get clothes for them, and food. Try to help the ones who are pregnant, or sick."

"She's a trench worker," I think: "It's the Flanders Fields of Social Work." Anyone can service nice, clean, proper middle class families of Houston or Portland or Chicago. There are thousands of Ph.D.s and M.S.W.s who will "intervene" with the rich of Hillsborough, or Cambridge, or the Upper East Side. Problems in yuppie Atlanta, San Francisco, Seattle? Let me at them!

But the poor of Mexico? Perish the thought. It's too hot and smelly in there. We have another weekend workshop to set up in Boulder, Cedar Springs, Airlie. We're just too busy to help out — sorry, we have some clients flying in from Hawaii. And we just raised our rates last week. And then in a month we'll be skiing in Vail. We might be able to do something later, maybe next year or the year afterwards.

Mexicali Jail! It's the place where the knowledge gleaned at this conference will be placed in the crucible, maybe even shown to be wanting. What can the theories of Freud mean to the malnourished of Northern Mexico? How are the genteel interventions of Satir, Masterson, Poulser or Carl Rogers going to be meaningful to those who live in the poorest jail in one the poorest areas of the world? Who are the IP's in a society that lives on the hillside, in shacks with no water, no electricity, no social security, no food stamps, no AFDC, no medicine, nothing but dark, stinking, putrescent poverty?

Those on the battlefields of Northern Mexico are there taking care of those that no one else will take care of. Maria, who got caught shoplifting at the Calimax. Juana, whose husband Miguel came home drunk, and beat her for the hundredth time, and she couldn't take it anymore, so she knifed him. She didn't mean to kill him. And O yes, bony Alicia. They caught her smuggling. But they also say that she has thirteen children, and the youngest have no clothes, no food, three of them sick with the dysentery.

I suppose that what Sister Angelica needs probably cannot be found at this conference. No: nor in this state. Perhaps not even in this country. We should write a letter to Sister Angelica's boss. Tell him how lucky he is to have someone like her, working in heat that would fell an ox, working without complaint, every day, journeying to La Mesa de Mexicali Jail, where the sour-faced guard lets her in, for the umpteenth time. She gives him a little of the bread, too, because he's not so well-paid either, and because he always lets her in. He doesn't have to.

Yes — it's time to send a letter. To see if we can get a few more clothes, some more food for the dispossessed, some more help for those at the bottom of the barrel of Mexicali. Get Sister Angelica another car, so the 1975 Gremlin she's been using (terrible transmission! It's a wonder that she makes it!) can be replaced. Get some more medicine for all the sick patients there in Mexicali jail.

"I know you get requests all the time, for help and such," I'll tell her boss. "But this is a very special project to me, as it might be to you, too. You might say that Sister Angelica is out on the front lines, trying to keep some of the poorest, most miserable, most wretched people in the world from absolute starvation, starvation of spirit, starvation of hope . . . "

I know it's a touchy subject but I'll bring it up anyway: "They say that you have there, in the most holy of cities, some ancient jewels, of centuries past. It would be something, wouldn't it, if we could take just one of these (a small tiara, say, from the seventeenth century or so) cash it in (I know a museum or two that would pay a pretty penny for an artifact from the reign of Pope Innocenti X) and then we could turn the money over to Sister Angelica, so she could get a little extra help in what is, after all, a hot, tiring, and thankless job. She could buy some extra medicine. She might be able to take off an extra day each week (if we can persuade her!) She could hire an assistant or two, social workers or teachers who could instruct her wards on how to take up some trade, so they'll have *something*, so they won't have to return to Mexicali Jail again and again. I'm sure you can trust her; she won't waste or squander the money, whatever we're able to come up with. And I don't think that your Museum will be any poorer — considering what the money will be going for. I'll bet that visitors to your city fifty or a hundred or five hundred years in the future would agree that by helping the poor of Mexicali Jail we might be creating something just as important as a bejewelled artifact from three hundred years ago, hidden in some dark storage room. I'm sure that they, the future visitors, would forgive us our trespass of helping the poor, the very very poor . . . "

I don't tell Sister Angelica about my letter-writing project on her behalf. I don't want to get her hopes up. But I do tell her that she's a star. I tell her I get to her neighborhood every now and then, and that I'd like to have a chance to travel over to the jail with her, see how she's doing, maybe lend a hand. And — just like that — she gives me a shy and motherly hug. "It's the first time I've been hugged by a nun," I tell my friends later.

PART II

Virginia Satir

CHAPTER 7

During my analytic training, I also knew Frieda Fromm Reichman. She was a remarkable person. She used to wear this beat-up white coat because all good doctors in those days wore white coats. She used to have the pockets stuffed with candy. She used to go around giving schizophrenics candy. She's the one from whom I learned that delusions occupy time and space, and there's only room for one person. So if the therapist gets into it, the patient has to get out of it. This was all in the days before tranquilizers, and the patients used to do awful things. They'd defecate in the middle of the floor. She'd find a patient playing with his feces, and she'd put on rubber gloves and get down on the floor and play with the patient's feces. The patient would stop. The patient wouldn't do that anymore. She was a very, very warm person. She used to say that there's no such thing as a hopeless patient; there are only hopeless techniques and we have to discover new techniques.

— Nick Cummings[11]

Q. I'd like to ask you about the homeless population in the states. We're putting a lot of emphasis on the homeless population and all the mentally ill people roaming the streets. Is this because we have more mentally ill people today, or is it that we recognize it more?

Laing. It is, I think, a very American idea that you've got to be ill in order to prefer to live in a park, or in a street, than inside of a house. We hear of London in Dickens' time, where you had to step over abortions in the pavement, and discarded babies. People died outside, and many people lived outside, and wandered around . . . . It was regarded as a normal part of society.

Whitaker. What I think Ronnie is talking about is the difference in the community's relationship with them. Because it wasn't — what? — fifty years ago when one of the popular songs was "Hallelujah! I'm a bum. I went to a house, and knocked on the door, lady came out, said I'd been there before." You were respected for personhood. And the fact that you weren't willing to get in line and put together automobiles, like everyone was supposed to, was seen as a proof of your maturity. Nowadays, you can't even be a person in the sense of raising children; you're supposed to get out and produce money for the social structure. It's materialism carried to a ridiculous extreme.

Q. Isn't there something wrong with these people in a social context? Should we ignore them or what should we do for them?

Whitaker. I admire them, but of course that's *my* problem.

Q. Is that what you'd like to do?

Whitaker. Of course.

Q. Why don't you?

Whitaker. I want to earn money, and I'm a sociopath like most of the rest of us. And I would not want to be hungry, and to be cold at night. But I wouldn't mind sleeping in the foyer of the church or the lounge of the gymnasium. I think I'd be lonesome for some more loving contact, but that might be a hell of a lot more fun than being in this kind of rat race that we're all in.

Q. Where does therapy fit in with these kinds of people?

Whitaker. Well, that's an issue that's very tricky. Is therapy something that we offer them if they ask for it, or something that we force on them because we want them to capitulate? The question of how to be a good foster mother is the question of how to be a good therapist. And I think you need to set up with the foster child the rules for your household and his rights: "I'm glad to be your foster mother, the judge told me I was supposed to, and you can't shit in the middle of the living room floor. You can take things out of the refrigerator, but not so much that we won't have enough for dinner. And you must remember that I love my own children more than I do foster children. And you better not get between me and my husband when we have a fight. But you can call the judge tomorrow and tell him you don't like the place and he should take you out. You can call your mother whenever you want to. You can cuss at me freely if I don't lose my temper. And you can run away anytime you want, but I'll call the judge because that's my duty. But I won't chase you. And I would probably (pause) like your coming back. And I hope we can get to be loving friends, because I would not want to go on having you around if you and I just piss each other off endlessly." (Pause). That's the way I think about therapy.

■ ■ ■

One of the ongoing themes of the "Evolution of Psychotherapy Conference" is success: the sweet report of success that comes in the tales of this or that patient or client who was changed, improved, *cured*: "After that, I knew she wouldn't be suicidal." "She started eating again after our session." "When I saw the boy seven years later, he was healthy and active." "The child was no longer considered to be a problem, and the parents stopped talking about divorce."

With all these testimonials, those who refer to it as the "Woodstock of Psychotherapy" are using the wrong terminology. No — they should be calling it the "Lourdes of Psychotherapy," as in the place in the Pyrenees where the Virgin Mary came down to move the stars in the heavens and perform miracles for the young, beautiful, and faithful Bernadette. "Maybe they should be selling Miracle Cure Kits," I think, and then see that they are doing exactly that. The kits aren't filled with Lourdes water — they are filled with words. They're called books. They have titles like *Healing in Hypnosis*, *Helping Families to Change*, *The Situation is Hopeless, but Not Serious*. And if you buy one and thrust it at your favorite miracle worker, you might get a signature.

It's the Lourdes of Arizona, isn't it? Twenty-six of the holies, together with seven thousand of the supplicants, gathered together on the deserts of Arizona in December of 1985 to talk about the Morphology of Miracles — and what a place to meet! It's a desert in the middle of a city in the middle of a desert.

They selected this place in the desert for the miracles to bloom, and why not? There is no water nor life here: Phoenix is a city that was created not by logic but by black magic. We don't care if there is no life or water or plants here: we'll fabricate them all. We'll create a hole of light out of the darkness, and then give it the name of the miraculous bird that makes *a nest of spices, sings a melodious dirge, flaps its wings to set fire to the pile, consumes itself in the ashes, but comes forth with a new life to repeat its former one.*[12]

Phoenix, on its yellow nest of sand, surrounded in winter by the cold blasts of the heavens — ice winds that keen out of the Vulture Mountains, winds so chill that they cut you to the bone. And, contrarywise, in bleak summer, a fire set with such force and ferocity that you find yourself panting in the accumulated BTUs — coming at you with such power that you think your breath is being hacked from your lungs. You leave your house in the morning, race from house to car, the car where the black seats singe your very bum, and your breath sears your lungs, this godforsaken Phoenix (name it Furnace Creek! Hell's Half-Acre! The Devil's Kitchen!) Give it back to the burrowing owls and the creosotes and the ocotillos and jackrabbits, the snakes and scorpions and gila monsters; a place, not, god knows, for the 1,000,000 humans who move here from Chicago or Buffalo or Massachusetts or Maine, move onto the barren mesas to pretend that here is a city, here is civilization, here is culture and knowledge.

■ ■ ■

In their press conferences the faculty members interact with thirty or so media representatives, with each other, with their fantasies of themselves, and their fantasies of the "press." This gives us a chance to view Albert Ellis, conjoined with his opposite, the amiable and soft-spoken Judd Marmor of Los Angeles. There is, too, the union of veteran family therapist Virginia Satir with the learned

Bruno Bettelheim. Best, there's the meeting between R. D. Laing, the urbane therapist from Scotland (who is, as well, an elegant poet), and Carl Whitaker, one of the sharpest practitioners of family therapy and a delightfully eccentric M.D. from Wisconsin.

Having these two together for an hour was not unlike witnessing a tennis game at your local country club between, say, John McEnroe and Boris Becker, serving up "just a friendly game or two." The psychodynamic volleys between Laing and Whitaker, each to each, then out to our end of the room, were glittering and fun. We recorded their session, and I remember thinking at the time that it was an interesting dialogue; now I see that it's not unlike Antonioni's *Blow Up*. Each playback seems (it *seems*: one can't be too sure) to create some new artistry of words and concepts that passed us by at the time of the recording.

The dummies sent in as representatives of the Phoenix newspapers and radio and television stations didn't seem too impressed, however, and their questions were of the "Unh, what *is* the role of psychology, unh, in the eighties?" and "What do you think of Phoenix?" school of base reporting. Others of us felt that — especially in the Laing/Whitaker and Satir/Bettelheim pairings, we were privileged viewers at an hour-long tête-a-tête between major savants of modern psychotherapy — much as if we had been allowed to join in and ask questions at one of those fabled meetings of Alan Watts and Carl Jung, or Aldous Huxley and Milton Erickson, or Ezra Pound and T. S. Eliot.

■ ■ ■

Murray Bowen was born in Waverly, Tennessee at the beginning of the century. Without a doubt, he is the

Brahmin of Family Therapy. He has been practicing his own special study of it at the Georgetown University Family Center for twenty-six years. He is pink faced, old, cadaverous, bent. An operation on his throat has given his voice a sepulchral quality. He speaks with the same authority as Bruno Bettelheim, and even when his words are not compelling in content, they carry a force that comes from a man who has been a leader in an important, revolutionary school of psychological change. No less than Freud, Jung, Alfred Adler, Fritz Perls, and Otto Rank, it is Bowen who is most cited as the leader by the Young Turks.

Still, it seemed that his earliest speech was a disappointment to many of the folk who had come to hear the stars. It was a speech on the history of Talk Therapy — the experience of talking out a problem with a compassionate other — the healing process of words. The presentation was given in Exhibit Hall B, a mammoth area capable of seating 10,000 people (with room for a small cafeteria at the back.) Partway through the speech, I went for a cup of coffee. The dozen loudspeakers in the room, each in cabinets twenty feet tall, carried Bowen's voice throughout, but given the physics of sound interference and echo, his words would turn, and phase in and out as I moved through them. A strange experience: a frail, old man, with frail old words, words on the therapy of speech over the millennia; his words like starlings, turned one upon the other in that immense cavern of a lecture hall.

It put me in mind of a cathedral I visited in Málaga some quarter century ago. It was huge and cold, with a roof that vanished far in the distance making it impossible to gauge the scale of it, the voice in Latin sounding and ebbing off itself so that it carried its own magic, a magic which had nothing to do with the man in his chasuble, speaking the obscure prayers of the ages, for the supplicants everywhere. In the same way, a frail priest of catharsis speaks to us out of prehistoric time with a voice which is something greater than a voice, rumbling through so many thousands of cubic feet of space, a voice out of our pasts of holiness.

Like many old old people, Bowen has the feel not only of one who has lived, but of one who is ready to move on. Some say his speech here (entitled "Psychotherapy: Past, Present, and Future") was his swan song to the profession to which he had given so much. It was Bowen who had conceived of "the three generations" framework — that worthwhile family therapy should include not only mother, father and children, but grandparents, grandchildren, and "significant others" as well.

It was Bowen who pioneered the concept of "fusion" — a function of "schizophrenic families." Vincent Foley writes that Bowen hypothesized that there are whole families in which members "are related to each other in such a way that none of them has a true sense of self as an independent individual." The boundaries between the family members come to be blurred, and "the family forms into an amorphous mass without distinguishing characteristics. Family members can neither gain true intimacy, nor can they separate and become persons. They have a quality of *fusion* that gives them no freedom or option to move closer or to get away."[13]

Radical thinking. Not only individuals, but whole families can develop psychotic patterns, and by this process, can establish and reinforce psychoneuroses. A family can become manic or borderline psychotic. The much touted family, the ideal unit of Western society, is often dreamily pictured with smiling faces around the Christmas tree; dad reading comics to the kids on Sundays; mother, father, gramps, granny, and the children sitting around the table on Thanksgiving. Yet Bowen says that under the right (or wrong) conditions, the system turns poisonous, dark, and oppressive. Hatred, violence, destruction, and suicide can be the product of families that are too loving, *too* wrapped up in each other. Those familiar with the plays of Eugene O'Neill should not find this concept surprising nor radical.

▪ ▪ ▪

For this conference, Bettelheim and Bowen are our voices from the past, as surely as if Freud had risen up with cigar in hand, moving his beetle brows to address one of the workshops; or if a dour Jung had turned up to participate in a panel on dreams; or if Adler had come to tell us the experience of his own form of Family Therapy in 1922.

But it is Bowen who has an air of his own: his old man's voice; his soft southern accent; the knowledge of his having been there, having done it, being ready to exit. On the third day, as I go between the Phoenix Room and Exhibit Hall B, one of the participants stops me and says, "You should get to the Yuma Room as fast as you can, before the old man cacks." They are showing a videotape of Bowen talking about family therapy, and his theories, and his discoveries. The video is placed in near total darkness. He is turned from the camera so we can view, on screen, him as he sits, slumped over in his chair, looking not unlike Whistler's Mother. If you look very carefully, you can see another Bowen — a smaller, older version — the "real" Bowen, sitting motionless at the darkened podium, head forward, neck bent, as if in prayer or meditation, resting in the great weight of his thoughts. Above him, the giant image of himself on the screen, going on, in measured pace, saying "I want the family to be more detached." The Bowen-now is motionless, as is the Bowen-then. The two of them, speaking to us out of the past, from beyond the grave, speaking to us of works that have been done, done long ago, and are now done.

Zerka Moreno

CHAPTER 8

Q. Can you work with a symptom without knowing the cause?

Whitaker. I don't really care much about either. I just work with people, and I only do *that* because I enjoy it. And because they enjoy it.

Q. What do you do with somebody who doesn't do any of these things?

Whitaker. That's their problem. I just relax and go on with my life, and they're welcome to relax and go on with theirs . . . . I don't insist or even try to carry out the culture's demands of me to be the parent of everybody who shows up. They'll bite your tit if you're not careful.

Q. My question is, "How do people change?"

Whitaker. I'm more and more convinced that, in the first twenty years of seeing individual patients, I was very inadequate and very impotent. And I now like to let individuals sleep on the street or whatever they want. That's *their* life, and if they want me to help change their life, I insist on having other people in. I'm not interested in playing their breast-feeding mother.

Q. Other people in?

Whitaker. The rest of the family. Their mother and father, wife and girlfriend, homosexual partner, children, grandparents, the works.

Q. And what does that allow to happen?

Whitaker. It allows me to not make believe that I'm Superman. I tried that for a long while, and I didn't do so well.

Q. And by seeing the whole family?

Whitaker. Then I don't have to be *it.* They're it. And I'm trying to help this football team win games, rather than sleep with each other's wives, and frustrate each other's efforts to be a team.

▪ ▪ ▪

USA Today, showing a bit more awareness than the *Christian Science Monitor*, the *Washington Post*, NBC, ABC, CBS, UPI, and the Phoenix Bureau of the Associated Press, is at the convention in force. The *USA Today* Convention Fun-Pak comes complete with a questionnaire that goes to all 7,200 of the participants, asking such nosy questions as therapists' salary, age, experience, and success rate in therapy, which is not unlike asking a man of the cloth how many of his parishioners he has helped into heaven. I was thinking of taking one of the questionnaires and listing myself under the psychotherapeutic school of "None," with a 100 percent success rate, and a "$75,000 or more" salary scale, and under the "Comments" section, writing:

> *I find that the success of my practice is a direct function of deep, short-term sexual interventions with my clients. If we don't dally at least once a week, I think I am letting them down (or vice versa). They love it.*

It would be an appropriate tribute to a profession which in recent studies has been proved to have a higher rate of interpenetration than even the traditional consumer philanderers like icemen, milkmen, plumbers, or Fuller Brush men.[14] Such a letter printed in *USA Today* might signal the end of the psychotherapy we have come to know and love, not to say support, over the years.

■ ■ ■

The prophet of psychodrama is a lady called Zerka Moreno. Psychodrama is where you act out the roles of those (seen or unseen) who have influenced you in your life, from all perspectives. Thus, if you grew up as a fantasy child, (not who you were but who your parents *wanted* you to be,) then you get on stage and *become* a fantasy child, and then the child you really are. (You also get to become your parents). According to all reports, it is a moving and powerful experience for those in it, or even watching it. However, Ms. Moreno is more than a little bit dogmatic in her beliefs, caustic in her delivery, and final in her judgments. Her response to Minuchin's first speech (she was what was called a "discussant") was so bitter, some might even say jealous, that several members of the audience reacted noisily. One got up and said that he was appalled that she so "lacked compassion" in her presentation.

Moreno is also given to extended accolades of her long dead husband, one J. L. Moreno, the founder of psychodrama. At one point, Carl Whitaker naughtily asked her, in a panel, when she was going to go ahead and bury him. (One of Whitaker's most famous apothegms comes in consultation with a family in which the husband works eighteen hours a day. Whitaker asks, in apparent guilelessness, "When did you decide to divorce your wife and marry your job?")

■ ■ ■

There is a bulletin board in the main hallway of the Center. Under "H-I-J," I insert the following notice:

Dear Carl,
All is lost. What do we do?

Sigmund.

And under "E-F-G:"

Dear Sigmund,
What do you mean "we," white man? Have you thought of seeking professional help? I understand that boy Minuchin is a whiz.

Carl J.

■ ■ ■

Q. How do people change, how do people come to change?

Virginia Satir. O.K. First bear in mind — *everything I tell you, I make up.* Now, change means you're in a different place, but it doesn't say if it's better or worse. It merely means that the status quo has been interrupted. I need two things if someone tells me they want change. I need to interrupt the status quo, and I need to access things that will be harmonious to that person — whatever those things are.

Many times people don't have the vaguest idea what change is about. When you think about it, people change because they're in terrible pain, but sometimes people elect to stay just how they are.

The process of interfering with the status quo, developing new models, developing new hope, becomes a really difficult thing. That comes about because I move people's belief about what they have.

My modeling of people helps them to do some changing, but I'm aware that it's the hardest thing in the world. You have to remember that when someone's at Stage A, they don't know what Stage B is like. Everyone who asks for change is going into the unknown. And that's the scary part. There needs to be lots of support for that.

Virginia Satir likes to say that when she is counseling, she is really "sculpting." She is one of the earliest practitioners of Family Therapy — but despite the *Los Angeles Times' ex cathedra* statement that appeared the week after the conference, she is hardly "the Columbus of family therapy." The Cortez or the Magellan, yes; the Columbus, no.

In a video presentation in the Ballroom, she shows herself working with a family in which the father is 6′8″ tall. Satir is a believer in the destructive force of distancing. She wants her clients to see eye to eye. So she has the whole family — father, considerably shorter mother, fifteen-year-old son (the Identified Patient), and nine-year-old sister, move about, stand here and there, stand together and apart, look each other in the eyes, get sister between father and mother, and brother between sister and mother. Satir has blocks to stand on, some of greater, some of lesser height. She uses a technique familiar to the gestaltists, Ericksonians, and other family therapists — using concrete space, or lack of it, to reshape and reframe the family relationships. (She even briefly refers to a short stepladder she has used for couples of different heights. She calls it "the screwing stool." I was unable to track it down at the Hyatt Gift Shop or in the Convention Book Stall.)

Satir also asks the parents and children to "give each other forgiving messages" as they move about. She is very aware, as most wise therapists are aware, that the fifteen-year-old may be defined by the family as "the problem," but, in truth, he is merely acting out; he becomes an early warning system of destructive patterns of the other members of the family.

Satir knows instinctively how far she can push (and push around) each of the family members. In reality, she is doing Positional Therapy, but with a sensitivity to what can and cannot be affected. Thus as the "healing" session draws to a close, she says that she is able to make the son touch hands with the other members of the family, though asking him to go further (to hug, for example) would have been wrong. "It's all right to offer choices," she says, "but you don't want anyone to feel compelled."

At one point, the video tape of the family with Monster Man and Red the Renegade goes into fast forward. We see the whole family and Virginia, hustling about at high speed, stepping up and then down like jackrabbits, or like they were in a Buster Keaton movie, hugging and pulling away on the double, racing about the room at rocket velocity. "A wonderful metaphor for the whole helping profession," I think: "They all want to cure families like this in record time. This must be what instant psychotherapeutic salvation would look like."

A. A. Lazarus

CHAPTER 9

Even though there are some visibly eccentric therapies represented at the conference, there are others which have been left out, either by design or because, perhaps, even in contemporary psychotherapy, we do have our limits. For instance, there is something called Provocative Psychotherapy which is described in Corsini's book[15] as follows:

> [A therapist says to a client]:
>
> *"You talk like a slut; you dress like a slut; you walk like a slut and you look like a slut."*

Or:

> *"I am going to teach you how to be joyfully sadistic."*
>
> *"What's that?"*
>
> *"How to inflict pain on others and get to love it."*

As the author describes it:

> *This method of psychotherapy depends on humor as the major therapeutic modality, attempting to make the client see the ridiculousness of his thinking and acting, to "spit in his soup" as an Adlerian might say, so that once the client sees the stupidity of his thinking he will no longer be able to enjoy the nonsensical behavior of the past.*

Then there is something called Z-Process Attachment Therapy which is described in the following fashion:

> *The client comes into a room, and seated at two facing benches are eight people, four on a side. The client is induced to lie down on his or her back on the laps of the eight people who now hold the client firmly by the arms, legs, and body. The person at the top left is the therapist, who wraps his left arm around the client's head, and during the interview may tickle the patient's rib cage in an attempt to infuriate the client so that the client will go into a rage. Meanwhile, the client is helpless to move, being held down firmly by the therapist and the other seven people, who usually are friends and family members.*

As I say, even with the full representation of what Minuchin called "Zulus and Eskimos" at the conference, Dr. Robert Zaslow, inventor of "Z-Process Attachment Therapy," was not in attendance. He was not demonstrating, on stage, in Ballroom B, client cuddling, stroking, wrapping, tickling, enragement, or infuriation.

▪ ▪ ▪

A lot of psychotherapists suffer from psychophobia. That's fear of the mind.

— R. D. Laing

A. A. Lazarus, of South Africa, is the founder of something called Multimodal Therapy. He has created a device for the understanding of MMT. It's BASIC-ID, as in Behavior, Affect, Sensation, Imagery, Cognition, Interpersonal, and Drugs Biology. His presentations are filled with strange graphs and ratings and quasi-technical foo-foo-raw based on Basic ID, the whole of which uses big words, and is heavy with success stories.

In watching Lazarus, I catch myself wondering how anyone in the helping profession could look so spiffy, so orderly, be so well-manicured, so — well — so *anal.* He appears to be the Tom Wolfe of therapists, at least he is far more perfect in dress and speech than anyone else here: Blue shirt perfectly pressed; dark jacket, perfectly pressed; dark tie, perfectly pressed; white collar, perfectly pressed, perfectly cleaned; pink face, perfectly ordered; white hair, perfectly combed. I know if I get under the conference table (Should I do that? Should I check on his lower multimodals?) I'll find shoes perfectly polished, pants perfectly creased, socks perfectly clean. What is he trying to tell us? All of us with our disheveled neuroses; he with his perfect neobehavioristic patterns?

Lazarus may pretend to be a world apart from Albert Ellis, but they share a certain indulgence with the English language. This, by Lazarus, as description of his work:

> *The theoretical eclectic tends to draw from diverse systems that may be epistemologically incompatible, whereas the technical eclectic uses procedures drawn from different sources without necessarily subscribing to the theories or disciplines that spawned them. The upshot is a consistent, systematic, and testable set of beliefs and assumptions about human beings and their problems, and an armamentarium of effective therapeutic strategies for remedying their afflictions.*[16]

"Maybe Ellis and Lazarus are the same person," I think. "Maybe they are putting some great joke over on us." Yes, that's it. We've got a genuine clinical ambivert here, a *bona fide* dual personality. Sometimes he's ill-dressed, ill-mannered Albert Ellis with his New Yorker's hyperbole, that nonsense about Real Estate Investment Therapies, that bizarre language (and those klutzy songs!). Then, when no one is looking, he slips into the telephone booth (or into an Orgone Box) and emerges as Arnold Lazarus, of perfect attire, perfect South African accent, perfect face, with all those fifty-cent words, words like "synthesis," "multidimensional," "epistemological," and the give-away, the ever present, ever baffling "armamentarium." Rowdy Ellis and Proper Lazarus, once they get back into their box, or hotel room, or armamentarium, can indulge in endless dialogue with each other, occupying, as they do, the same brain pan, talking on and on about MMT, RET, CBT, Basic ID.

Obviously the whole meeting is turning me into a dingbat, if not a melancholic sociopath. When I repair to the eatery in the Conference Center with my 3,500 peers for a luncheon of chicken glue in leathern shell with smushed rice, they push me one notch further along towards the borderline by having The Cactus Plant Contest. The man with the microphone says we have to look under our chairs, and if there is a yellow dot stuck to the underside of it, we win the cactus plant which has been residing in the middle of the table for all these awful meals. I know it is another one of those anxiety producing psychological challenges devised by Milton Erickson's ghost to get us to lose weight, rid ourselves of headaches, stop drinking, nagging our husbands, and belittling our wives. I know mind tricks when I see them: How can you indulge in antisocial behavior patterns when you are busy crawling about on your hands and knees, looking at the bottoms of folding chairs (and the bottoms of your fellows!) for mythic yellow seals? And if you win, and they give you the plant — what you have to do is to start worrying about carrying an open bowl with eight pounds of

Arizona sand, *all in your suitcase*. One false move by the porter and you have a year's worth of desert in blouse, bra, and panty hose. I know instant cure when I see (or hear) it. The helpers who came here to learn about autism and valetudinarianism are going to get more than they bargained for, and they don't even know it yet.

Carl Rogers

CHAPTER 10

The owl of Minerva flies only at dusk.

— F. Nietzsche

There is a final panel on the "History of Psychotherapy" that I don't want to miss. The panelists are Rollo May, Carl Rogers, Thomas Szasz, and Carl Whitaker. Many of us have come from far away to see these masters, to have them teach us — not through the pasty words of books, not in film or video or sound recording but alive, in the flesh, talking their talk and walking their walk and best of all, *interacting with each other*. Only death, holocaust, or some other major event could keep me from this panel — but indeed, there was such a major event, totally unplanned for and out of the blue, that delayed me almost an hour so that I was unable to hear much of the panel. I'll explain all this further on.

Rogers and Whitaker use their time for reminiscing, Rollo May for some philosophizing. Obviously fresh from a reading of Barbara Tuchman's *A Distant Mirror*, May says that our own time is not unlike that of the 14th Century. "That is why there are so many of us therapists," he says:

"The upheaval of the times means that all our myths are gone, and we have no myths with which to replace them." How pleasant and restful his voice! Years ago, in one of my other incarnations (as a radio station programmer), I came across a dozen tapes he had made. He speaks with a cultured, deep, rich, sensuous, Midwestern accent. And as he tries to enlighten us on the world of myth, and on what they call (so grandly) Existential Psychotherapy, I realized what an important part the sonorous voice played in convincing us, as we all must be convinced at one time or another in our lives, that this was *it*: Rollo May had discovered the secret of the mind, what made it work, what made it right, what made it wrong. The old seducer! Listening to him at age seventy-five, even as his voice is dipping into old age, is still a voluptuous experience, like getting into the warm mineral bath that steams out of the side of the glacier and feeds into an icy mountain brook — a safe, lickerish bath there at the edge of a cold and brutish world. That's what it's like to listen to Rollo May.

Carl Rogers, on the other hand, decides to tell us some personal stories out of his past. He says, "I've never had a mentor, never had a supervisor. Indeed, all I have learned I learned from my clients." He doesn't deny the importance of his fellow workers, but he is claiming (as most good therapists claim) that his knowledge came from people who paid him to help them.

Rogers, in his sunset years, is still a controversial figure. His Center for the Studies of the Person in La Jolla is often wracked by controversy and dissention. As with his tenure at the Western Behavioral Sciences Institute, there seems to be a special type of anger that revolves about Rogers. It is almost that his nondirective sympathetic self draws a full complement of vampires and bats to it, like a light left illuminated at night to guide the way will pull a variety of winged beasts into its orbit. It is a sensitive note for those who know him and care for him.

Perhaps those very troubles have caused Rogers to launch other controversial pursuits of a more spiritual nature. There is his interest in world peace, for which he went to Central Europe to converse with diplomats of both East and West. In meetings, he talks with them about international conflict, much as if he were talking with individuals about their personal conflicts. The results, it is said, are surprising and hopeful.

What's more, he has shown (as has Laing) an interest in Eastern philosophy, previous lives and matters of the spirit. For the respected clinician and founder of "Rogerian Therapy" to take up such endeavors would not be unlike the Pope, in his dotage, taking up shamanism; or Jerry Falwell, as he gets older and dumber, going into necromancy. One is forced to always admire Rogers, as a man who is unafraid of the controversial — unafraid to admit to people his flirtation with international affairs, and exotic spiritualism.

In his presentation, Carl Whitaker says that he learned much from Ruth Mellor,[17] a social worker at the Louisville Child Guidance Center in 1941. "Ruth taught me the simplicity of human relating," says Whitaker: "After awhile, I began to sense that depression was kind of relative." Whitaker claims to have learned not only from his patients, but from the many experimental clinics that he studied at. "I fed patients on my lap with a baby bottle. I physically wrestled with my patients. I went through three years of saying nothing, just looking at them eyeball to eyeball. I was perfectly trained," he says: "I studied OB/

GYN, but then fell in love with schizophrenia."

Whitaker said a few more things to shock those convention-goers who had not already been put under by his ideas. "One thing that I learned is that there is no such a thing as murder — just a two-person collaboration." Or: "I found out that there is no lying to patients. Schizophrenics can see right through you. What the patients say about their own progress is vital — because it will be the truth."

And Whitaker was, as far as I was able to discover, the only one of the faculty to admit occasional defeat. "I had a patient in one of those luxurious sanitoriums for the very wealthy," he says. "And he hadn't left his bed for fifteen years, hadn't said a word for fifteen years. One day I was passing his room, and I said 'Would you like to play a game of ping-pong?' He got up and went to the ping-pong table. Beat the hell out of me. Every day after that, we played ping-pong for an hour. We did it for a year. He stayed in bed the rest of the time. He didn't get any better — never even talked to me. But he won every game."

■ ■ ■

Szasz was having nothing to do with philosophizing or reminiscing. He was ready — even on this panel of distinguished colleagues — to do some more proselytizing, some more ankle biting. One might say he was a man obsessed with a single subject, that is, the misfortunes attendant on giving any priesthood (in this case, psychiatrists) too much power. He reminds one of the village radical who may have studied Marx or Lenin or Engels just a bit too much and who is reluctant to go on to other endeavors in the path of life.

Szasz started in by claiming that he had it on good

authority that *Time* magazine's report on the conference would carry a picture of Jung's, Freud's, and Adler's grandchildren.[18] "It's mythology," he says: "The fact that the three of them are together here has nothing to do with illness or therapy. They are missing the point."

As one listens to and reads Szasz's words, one is struck by his continuing elegant commitment to freedom. He cites Benjamin Franklin, Thomas Jefferson, and James Madison, as well as the Bible, Talmudic history, and the Journal of the American Psychiatric Association. He sees the leaders of psychiatry in this country as constructing a theocracy in which heretics are punished by hospitalization, shock therapy, and forced restraint. The title of his formal talk at the conference was "Justifying Coercion Through Theology and Therapy."

He views the Old Testament as a work that is preoccupied with "power and powerlessness." (He also points out that the Bible views slavery as "a divinely ordained arrangement.") "To spread the benefits of Christianity and of psychiatry, no laws or limits need be observed: The end is so lofty that it justifies any means," he says: "How else can we account for the Christians killing heretics with the love of Jesus on their lips? How else can we account for psychiatrists imprisoning 'mental patients' with the Love of Mental Health on their lips?"

Szasz states that he has "rejected the idea that there exist illnesses of the mind or psyche" and attempts to "reëmphasize the definition of disease as a bodily, material phenomenon." He speaks of the "fraud and force, the deceptions and coercions, that pervade psychiatric practices . . . . I maintain that involuntary psychiatric interventions are not cures but coercions and urge that psychiatrists reject such methods." Perhaps the central thesis of

Szasz's thoughts comes towards the end of his talk:

> *Today, the psychiatrist is empowered not only to provide services to those who want them but also to persecute, in the name of mental health, those who do not want them. Faced with this situation, we have three basic options: We can take away the psychiatrist's power (to incarcerate the innocent or exculpate the guilty), we can take away his tools (lobotomy, electroshock, or neuroleptic drugs), or we can leave things as they are. Leaving things as they are would be like continuing to support a status quo of forcing 'help' on people in the name of God: We would continue to prattle about the 'rights of mental patients' as if heretics could have rights in a theocratic society; and we would congratulate ourselves on our humanitarian laws guaranteeing the 'mental patient's right to treatment,' as if inquisitors had ever wanted to deprive heretics of their right to worship the God of their persecutor.*

As one listens to Szasz, one wonders if his enthusiasm for battle might not be a bit misplaced. He is fighting a war that was essential when he published his first book[19] — but perhaps now there are other battles to be fought, others to be won. In California at this time, for example, a therapist is required to notify the police when a patient talks about illegal acts that he or she may be committing, or *planning* to commit. As a psychologist friend of mine said: "The police are in the therapy room with me all the time now, and many of my clients don't know it until I tell them." Some workers are not wise enough to warn their clients beforehand. Szasz's references to lobotomies and insulin therapy — as vivid and pressing as these malfeasances may once have been — do not acknowledge the enormous change in client-therapist relationships and techniques.

Szasz is a driven outsider. For Whitaker, Rollo May, and

Carl Rogers, controversies, battles, and revolutions are almost done. They can, at a conference like this, tell stories, (some enlightening, some funny, some regretful) of their past, of their work in bringing therapeutic intervention into the present, rather than leaving it in the past. For Szasz, the battle is ongoing, present, unchanging.

Jay Haley

CHAPTER 11

As I am on my way to this panel, I drop into the press room to tell Stan Smith to "take the rest of the day off." Smith is the Director of Public Relations for the conference. With his white hair, moustache and eyes right out of the clear winter's sky of Arizona, he looks just like some Hollywood casting agent's dream of the Daily Scribe. He is so omnipresent that I am constantly advising him to "take the rest of the day off," especially when I come into the press room late in the afternoon.

For the first time, he isn't there (maybe he *had* taken the rest of the day off). Instead, in a corner of the room, on a comfy couch, sits the Pundit of Psychosis, the Authority of Autism, the Master of Melancholia, Salvador Minuchin. Across from him is the *New York Times* in the form of reporter Daniel Goleman. Running into them like this is not unlike a rock fan chancing across Bruce Springsteen in heavy conversation with *Rolling Stone*, or for a litterateur to happen in on Eugene Ionesco being interviewed by the *Paris Review*. I remember thinking that Minuchin — hell, anyone — would be at their best in conversation with the *Times*. He, like all of us, would use this opportunity to reach beyond the limits of his political/professional/social world into another wherein reside the million or so power brokers, intellectuals, writers, columnists, television reporters, politicians, bankers, publishers, psychiatrists — the socially, financially, and culturally wealthy top bananas in America who indulge in a daily read of the *Times*.

Now despite what you may think to the contrary as you read this sea of words, I want you know that I am basically a shy (some would say reclusive) personality. I am not the type to barge in and shake hands with Minuchin and Goleman, introduce myself, join in with a bit of good-natured camaraderie, a well-placed joke or two, "You know, this conference puts me in mind of that old poem,

Roses are red
Violets are blue,
I'm a schizophrenic
And so am I."

Or maybe I could have said "Do you remember the one about the patient who thought he was a dog?" Pause, and then, with perfect timing: "The analyst said, '*Get off the couch!*'" Big burst of laughter, much gleeful nodding of heads, and I become an intimate part of the give-and-take going on between the newspaper of newspapers and the therapist of therapists.

Well, what I *really* do, shy snoop I am, is to get myself over to the far side of the room, pull out my notebook, and eavesdrop with a vengeance.

"There is an interesting interaction between the 7,000 people here and the twenty-six faculty," says Minuchin. "There is a kind of hope that those who are listening to us are more flexible than we are, that their perspectives will be effectively changed in their own way. Yesterday, I was on a panel with Moreno, Golding, and Ellis. And I realized that I was talking about what I was *thinking*, not what I was *doing*. I am unorthodox in what I think, not in what I do. All the "Family Therapies" have a united system of action, but different techniques.

"Now when I am with Dr. Masterson at a conference like this, I would never challenge him in person. Nothing good would come of a polemic. I might challenge him *in writing*, in a scholarly journal, but not here." Virginia Satir comes in, and chats pleasantly with one of the news people who has dropped in. "Don't they know what's going on?" I think. "How do you tell Virginia Satir to shut up?" I wonder. I would imagine this thought has bedevilled not a few of her clients.

"If you work with juvenile delinquents," says Minuchin, "you have to work within the context of not only the family, but the judicial system of the City of New York. There, the institutions, the approaches haven't changed for twenty years. This is something," he says slyly, "that might be developed by the *Times*.

"My thinking has gone beyond individuals. I am now worrying about how institutions deal with the needy as far as their problems go. A man came up to me here, said his sister was an anorexic, and had been institutionalized two years ago. It's too late for her now. She'll be very difficult to cure, because the institute will have made her a 'chronic.' An intervention (by a therapist) could have cured her in six months.

"The approaches we use to emotional problems don't change when we have a new piece of knowledge. *Knowledge does not expand the ability for dialogue*. We are prisoners of our dogma. We maintain our blindnesses. The diffusion of knowledge does not reverse systems." As I am writing, I fall into a brown study about the time I spent working on a master's degree in Social Work at a famous (but herein unnamed) California State University. The courses we took dealt with social issues, thinking, techniques — all from twenty-five years ago. One of the teachers had us reading Existentialism. In his assignments, he showed himself to be oblivious to the massive changes that Gregory Bateson, Systems Theory, Minuchin, Perls, and Erickson had created in the helping profession. Teachers are a product of their own schooling, and if these people are unwilling to read, understand, keep up with the revolutionary changes since 1960, they force us, their students, to study doctrines that were *outre* and formidable in the culture of the Eisenhower years, but which, in order to practice in the 1980s, are about as vital as brass hubcaps.

I was wondering if the *New York Times* was picking up on the wisdom that lay there, a jewel, ready to be snatched. Goleman looks like a middle-aged version of one of the Fabulous Furry Freak Brothers, the one with the beard and dark frizzy hair. His questions were monosyllabic, and his interjections tended to be of the "hum-&-um" order. I wondered if he heard the hooting of the owl.[20]

"We have to deal with the fiefdom of belief systems," said Minuchin. "Most conferences of the APA or group therapists come together with like-minded people and you can dance together in a ritual of confirmation with your priest. Here, there is a series of parallel monologues, not dialogue. And you need a generation to die before the ideas can die and you can have new ideas rise in their place.

"There's a strange love affair going on here," he said. "People come to those they know are going to die — people in the conference going up to Szasz and the other iconoclasts, asking for autographs. People say 'I love you' when we sign their books, and I feel like I am signing for the last time in my life. It's an interesting metaphor for the twenty-six faculty. What we need is a Ship of Fools: They could send us out on it and there would be a whole new generation not so tightly bound up in our models." His symbol is appropriate. In the early Renaissance, all the loonies would be gathered together and put on a boat that would drift up and down the Marne or the Seine, all the babblers locked together, safely out of the way of the other supposedly not-insane people.

"Psychoanalysis is so powerful," says Minuchin, "and so oversold. At the time when it came into being, the world was seen as safe: There was the illusion that the world was permanent, that there would be no changes. This was the context of psychoanalysis: 'Your perspective and your future will be directly related to your efforts.' You didn't have to worry about the *impermanence* of the world.

"We've learned now that individual power is not that important. And Family Therapy is part of that learning because what you have now is the difference in world view. Individual Therapy cannot exist in the world of today. We have so many changes to internalize and we don't know if the world will be here tomorrow. We have to become politicized because of our interdependence," says Minuchin, and he reminds me of the social workers in the jungle slums of Chicago and Philadelphia and New York in the 1920s. Jane Addams of Hull House, convinced that there was an interdependence of social justice with the possibility for change. A radicalism that grew out of their work, and the knowledge that the social system, the political system, and the internal psyche are all intertwined.

"We cannot look at our people without a model of our

time," says Minuchin. "The world is a ship in space. The individual used to be the center of therapy, but now our children, the mass media, politics, are all interconnected. Family Therapy connects us to our country.

"Psychoanalysis was optimistic, but it divorced one from the contexts. Family therapy deals with the world," he said. I was thinking of Bettelheim. He seemed to pooh-pooh much of Minuchin's thinking, and his aggressive technique. And yet, of all the people who should see psychotherapeutic thinking with a world view, he should be the one. After all, he personally experienced what happens when an intellectual class abandons its own society, leaves "politics to the politicians." His two years in a concentration camp certainly told him the price of isolation, the price of individualism that pure psychoanalysis connotes.

■ ■ ■

Q. Looking over this conference, what do you think are the ways in which the faculty here [is] coming together, and what do you think are the biggest divergences?

Laing. Well, they're not coming together, I'll tell you that.

Whitaker. I think the real divergence may be those people who want to help people get to where the therapist thinks they *could* be; and those people who want to help people be more of who they are, rather than somebody else. You could simplify that by making it a differential between "manipulators" and "enablers." I think that's oversimplistic, and I think that it may very well be that a lot of what therapists do is unknown to the therapists, and maybe a hell of a lot help without their knowing about what it is.

Q. Just like teachers never know?

Whitaker. Of course, of course. Or like my racket of getting grandparents in, and asking for their consultation in helping this family that consists of their daughter and her husband and their grandchildren. And hour after hour I can sit and listen to what seems like gobbledygook or social chitchat or very defensive stuff, and the next week when the nuclear family comes in, they say "Did you hear what my mother said?" No. "Well, I *never* heard her say anything like that before in my entire life." Grandmother didn't know what she was saying that made a difference to her daughter. And I sure as hell didn't hear anything that sounded significant. But the connection between those two people had been going on for forty years. And they [the children] hear things differently when they're forty than they heard them, and swallowed them, when they were six. So I think therapists are a lot like that. The foster mothers who say things that may not mean much to them, but may turn out to mean a hell of a lot — a symbolic experience — for the patient. So I don't know [that] the divergence is all that real. It's just very apparent sometimes.

PART III

Jeffrey Zeig

CHAPTER 12

Don't Just Do Something, Stand There

— Alma Menn[21]

I probably could be considered a fair example of the American system of psychotherapy at work. I visited my first therapist, a traditional Jungian, back in 1956. I was in trouble. I was haunted by a dark mood that wouldn't go away. As they say, I didn't have a clue. After a few weeks in which I bared what I thought was my soul, the therapist, a Quaker by the name of Dr. Clark, suggested that my depression might be caused by Unrequited Love. "Love? What love?" I said. "For your roommate." he said. I didn't believe him any more than I believed any other damfool of the time — resistance was strong — but now, so many years later, I would guess he was right. (It's a fine testament to the American educational system that I was twenty-two years old, a junior in a well-considered East Coast college, had read Shakespeare, Keats, Byron, Wordsworth, and many of the Pre-Raphaelites, indeed, was majoring in English poetry — and I still didn't know what the hell love was).

Since then, on and off, over the decades I have visited several other "counselors," "psychologists," "therapists," of all sorts of persuasions, with all sorts of degrees. I would like to attest here and now that I don't think I have been harmed by any of the M.D.s, Ph.D.s, and M.S.W.s that worked on me with me. To the contrary, I can't think of one of them who was not helpful to me in one way or another, and I can think of two who got me out of psychological holes which I considered, at the time, to be impossible to escape from.

Now this does not mean that I am without reservations about the Helping Profession. A relative of mine on the East Coast started seeing a Freudian psychoanalyst twenty-five years ago. The analyst began by prescribing large doses of psychotropic drugs. Sometime not long after, while she was still a patient, he seduced her. She stayed on tranquilizers throughout this period and for about ten years afterwards.

She is now, and finally, away from him. She is more or less off drugs, but she's still given to the head movements and lip smacking which are characteristic of *tardive dyskenesia* which afflicts those who are addicted to Thorazine and the like. Her other self-destruct tendencies are, to this day, considerable and ferocious. Her analyst, who wrought all this change, is still a respected member of the psychoanalytic profession. He has never been exposed for what (I assume) he has done to others besides her. I understand that he is still "practicing," writes extensively in the learned journals, is still magnificently protected by his colleagues of the American Psychoanalytical Association and the American Medical Association. I can only wish, in the days leading up to his much-to-be-wished-for passing on, that he might experience a touch of the grief that he has, in forty years of malpractice, wreaked on the naïve, the innocent, and the unprotected.

I was, as I say, far more fortunate. None of my therapists were in business to seduce me, nor harm me. Some were incompetent, by which I mean that they didn't have enough of the necessary combination of human compassion, brains, warmth, and caginess to get me out of whatever it was that had brought me to them in the first place. Some were just plain dull. Some were brilliant, recognizing all my tricks from the moment they met me (we all use tricks to defend our delusions — even when those delusions produce psychic pain).

I consider my journeys in and out of their various offices and thought systems as a pilgrimage. I also think that this journey is no more harmful than the journey of the wandering fool in Czarist Russia, or the poverty vow that takes some Indians a lifetime across their native land as sadhus, journeys that are traditional for the mendicants of Hinduism. My goal was neither more nor less meaningful than that of the Beats in their eternal car trips from New York to Denver to San Francisco, and back again. My wandering taught me no less than those of the European explorers who spent their lives on journeys into the heart of darkest Africa, or into the white and dismal wastes of Antarctica. That I chose to chase the will-o'-the-wisp in partnership with the practitioners of Jungian Therapy, Neuro-Linguistic Programming, Sensitivity Training, Reality Therapy, Gestalt Psychology, Transactional Analysis, Fisher-Hoffman Therapy, Rolfing, est, and neo-Rankians probably did no harm and surely gave me hope at a time when I desperately needed hope. The actual insights that came about are part of the accoutrements I now carry about with me on the remainder of this colorful journey through life, the world; time, space.

■ ■ ■

One of my journeys led me, seven years ago, into the office of Milton Erickson. It was long after he had given up private practice, and, as it turned out, shortly before he died. He was spending four hours a day in "seminar." That's what they called them. That's not what they really were. These are the notes I made at the time:

Milton Erickson moved to Phoenix in 1949 for his health. He lives in a tract house on 12th Street, in a polyglot, hapless looking part of the city. The meetings take place in a room that appears to be half kitchen, half living room. His wheelchair is crammed awkwardly through the doorway of the room where the ten us of are ranged. We are all sitting on 1955 Motel Moderne furniture which I doubt has changed any in the last decade. Erickson wears his famous purple robes (he is color-blind — the only color he can see is bright purple). He also wears a purple shirt, and purple knit booties, all of which make him look like a giant baby.

There are desert artifacts everywhere: skulls, stones, desert bird bones. The air conditioner (it is June) is noisy, and inefficient and cranky; and the traffic outside on 12th Street is just as noisy.

The doctor sits in his uncomfortable wheelchair — no footrests — on a giant foam cushion, his bootied feet scarcely touching the purple carpet set on the floor. He had polio twice: once in 1917 and again during the last great epidemic of the early fifties.[22] He has no use of his right hand and little of his left. His one motion is to lean forward awkwardly to observe the visitors, or to sit back uncomfortably, in his chair. He looks like a great stuffed panda with huge, glaucous, penetrating eyes.

He gives "audiences" — my words, not his own — six days a week to psychiatrists, psychologists, M.D.s, psychiatric social workers, and counselors who come from all over the continent to spend four hours in this room, listening to him — listening to him "tell stories."

It is hot and close in the room. Often, it is impossible to hear what he is saying. Not only does the traffic and air conditioner create too much ambient background noise, but polio has robbed Erickson of many of the muscles of throat, mouth, tongue, and lips. His words are difficult to hear, and often, he will go into coughing spasms — wheezing great, weak, indraughts of breath — so he sounds not unlike one on his death-bed. "Just my luck," I think. "I spend months angling to see him, and he dies on the first of the days I'm to be here." Since my coughs often sound the same, I have the cold comfort of imagining us going together into the mesmeric hereafter from this dingy, no exit room.

This is the master. It is an honor to be here. Thousands try, few get past the eagle eyes of his wife, who is also the reservations secretary. This is some feudal court out of the Ch'in Dynasty, and only the select out of the masses get to the court (some court!) of the wise man.

A whole industry has risen about visiting the Prophet of Phoenix. One comes for a day or two, and then advertises that one has "studied under Milton Erickson." This means you can charge $1,000 a day for seminars. Few pay attention to the fact that the master himself only charges $25 a day for visitors. I think I love him for that reason if for no other. He doesn't care about money, getting rich, making it in the American dream factory. He gives away information, knowledge, insights — gives them to all comers for so little.

His stories are Zen koans which follow each other without pause. Many of them are familiar. We have already read them in *Psychology Today*, or in the many articles he has authored himself, or in one of the many books about him by Jay Haley, Ernest Rossi, Jeff Zeig, or Bandler and Grindler[23] (two California heavies who are the Rosencrantz and Guildenstern of the Ericksonian movement). There are also dozens of videotapes floating around of hypnotic sessions, where you can watch him put people in trance, and they sit there unmoving, one hand frozen halfway between knee and face, and he mutters incomprehensible things to them, and they nod and smile or weep a little bit, and he mutters again, and they sit there motionless. These tapes are treasured by the followers of Erickson, but to some of us they are more like a weekend festival of repeated showings of *Last Year at Marienbad* alternating with Andy Warhol's eight-hour-long documentary footage of the Empire State Building.

Many who come to the sessions already know the punchlines of the stories he tells. But there is a difference in hearing them directly from his lips. His voice is so quiet, his lung power so shot with post-polio syndrome (a gradual weakening of the remaining muscles, decades after the original onslaught of the disease) that whole words, or sentences are sometimes lost in the babble of street noises and moving about the room.

No matter — half the audience seems to be in hypnotic trance. As Erickson speaks, he plays us like some great chromatic organ, putting this or that person into trance, keying words to one or another of us. And the whole thing is so subtle that I sometimes think nothing at all is happening. At other times, I am dead sure that this giant purple panda knows everything going on in the room, and is making some magic music with our minds and psyches, testing our *aqua vitae*, checking to see if our mental pumps are working, adjusting screws here and nuts there, then plunging with us into the pool of our souls, to come up with bits and pieces of our gossamer selves that don't necessarily belong in this dusty, stifling room in Phoenix, Arizona on one of the hottest days of June, 1979.

The stories ramble on in apparent random order. There is the one of the two nurses who think their husbands are "sexually perverted." There is another of the nurse who was required to squat over a mirror, so that she could learn to have intercourse. Her husband was required to learn how to masturbate, "to get an erection at will, and that's no man named Will." His stories use puns, and anagrams, and poetic techniques right out of Shakespeare, and are often just as obscure. Sometimes I catch myself thinking, "What am I doing here, listening to this nonsense?" This old man, an old man with glittering eyes — not unlike the eyes of some of the more frightening desert snakes. "I flew to Phoenix for *this*?" I think. "What would it be like if nothing were happening — nothing at all? Suppose we are so sucked in by his myth that we will believe anything?" I remember what I once read about people who were always trying to analyze his stories for some secret meaning. He called them "city slickers."

I am sweating on my Drugstore-Cowboy Naugahyde Chair, and there is a long confusing story about a man with claustrophobia who Erickson put in a closet, and he closes the door one millimeter, and the wall behind him, and he closes and opens the door, and closes the door, and opens it, and closes the door, and closes the door, and each time he says "close," I find my eyes closing, and I can not and do not wish to open them. I am in one of the famous Ericksonian trances and want to stay there as my mind struggles with trying to remember all his articles about telling stories with all those trance-inducing words in them, and of overcoming people's resistance to being put under. One of the ladies in the audience — sobbing — has found some secret grief in the story he is telling, a sadness stuck in it, clove-in-the-onion style, touching her in her deep trance. "She's getting something and I'm not," I think jealously. "I want it too." I remember when I forced myself to drag through two sequential weekends of *est*, so I could get It — and I remember not getting It, and thinking "What's wrong with me? Why can't I get It?"

At the break, I go into the bathroom, and steal some of the Ericksonian Aim for my breath, so I won't offend my seatmates when I go into the Ultimate Trance. I come back and stand about, trying to avoid that butt-breaking Naugahyde chair, and I am sort of dreaming, and I look at Erickson, at his eyes, so heavy-lidded, and they widen — all pupil, no iris, as he shoots a visual arrow at me, then down at the chair, a look that says "*Siddown Buster!*" and I do, with alacrity. Does he have that power because we all acknowledge that he is the master? Or is he the master because he has all that power?

Later, we visit his house next door. His coach-dog growls at me. There are purple gowns and white orthopedic corsets hanging on the clothesline. He has a purple telephone, and he writes in purple. Three of the seven in audience today wore purple in homage to him. He shows us photographs of children and grandchildren. I wonder what it would be like to grow up the child of Milton Erickson. He was probably one of the first professionals to propound the idea known by all good mothers that, as a parent, you never violate the experience of your child. He told Jay Haley about his son at age five, taking a bad fall down the back stairs.[24] Between the boy's screams, Erickson would say "That hurts awful, Robert, and it will keep right on hurting." He was confirming the child's feelings, instead of doing what so many parents do, those that say, "O, pooh — that doesn't hurt at all," confusing the child about what is being felt, against what some authority-parent says about what *should* be felt.

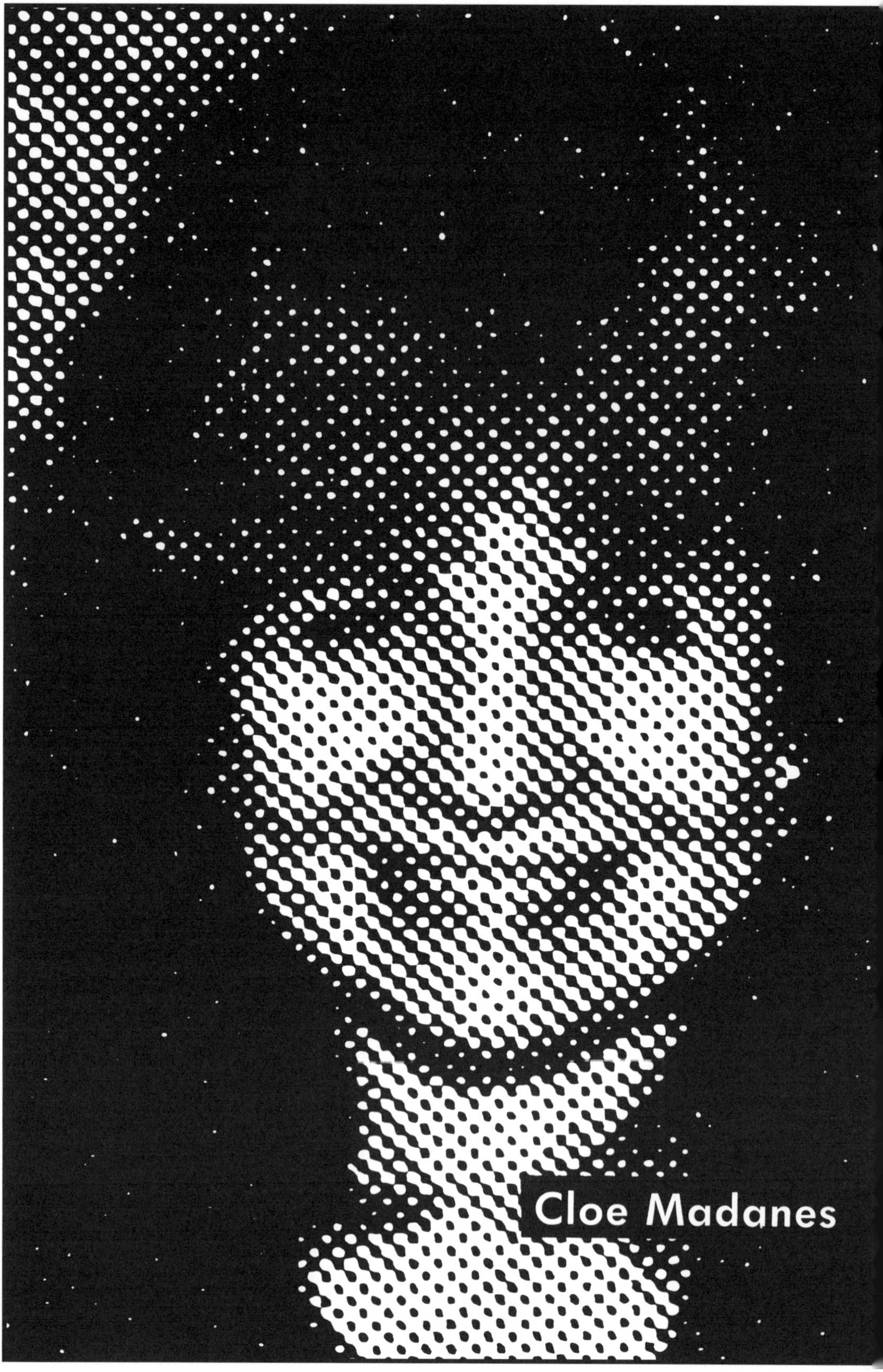
Cloe Madanes

CHAPTER 13

The Erickson house is filled with ironwood statues of dogs, octopuses, trees, ferns. My back hurts and so does my behind. I wish I could borrow a quick trance from him, have him tell me that it doesn't really hurt. What is it my friend Lorna says? — that Erickson spends three hours each morning reframing *him-self* in trance, because of his painful arthritis. I would probably be just as well off back at the hotel in the jacuzzi, breathing the air that makes me sweat so copiously in this hundred-and-ten-degree city which, I am beginning to think, doesn't belong here at all.

Cathy and Lorna have travelled here with me from California. They are *real* therapists, and are the ones who got me in the door. After we leave Erickson's, we go to the bar in the Arizona Biltmore. They tell me some stories about him. Like most fans, they have a good complement of them gathered over the years, some of which are unpublished. We settle into a booth near the door. There is a live chamber group playing "Just a Violet." At the bar, a young man with a camera challenges a man in tie and jacket to a fight. Seems cameraman thinks the other man was making goo-goo eyes at his girlfriend, or wife, or hooker.

"O no," I say. They go out into the hall, right next to where I am drinking my Molsons, and the cameraman kicks the feet out from under the well dressed fellow, and continues kicking him in the ribs, the back, the head, the face. "This is not happening," I think. "I'm still in a trance, aren't I?" I am in the elegant bar of the Frank Lloyd Wright designed Arizona Biltmore. There are ladies in long dresses, men in ties and formal jackets, waiters in tuxedos, and this American, macho brawl is happening right next to us out in the hallway. "Did you see how that woman played those two guys," says Cathy to Lorna, "played them just like a violin. Boy, you sure are scared," she says to me.

After the blood stops flowing and I come up from under the booth, I tell them about the old geezer who got into the hotel Jacuzzi with me this morning. This was the dialogue we had:

He: What happened to you?

Me: Polio.

He: When?

Me: O, twenty-five years ago.

He: You were born a cripple?

Me: No. I got polio twenty-five years ago. I ain't no spring chicken, you know.

He: What happened to you?

Me: What do you mean?

He: Didja have an auto accident?

Me: [Resigns].

Lorna and Cathy talk more about Erickson. Lorna, on her tenth visit to see him, says that he is somewhat nineteenth century in his attitude towards women. He has many stories about women who revolt, become independent — but who ultimately come back to marry, raise a family, be happy. He says they find "the cradle of the womb" — that is, the blessings of motherhood. Later, she sends me an article called "Myths About Erickson" by Corydon Hammond of the University of Utah. It demonstrates that Erickson was a more careful, practiced technician than most people realize. It also shows that what people perceived as "tricks" were more in the nature of common sense. It contains the following dialogue between Erickson and "one brave student:"

"Were you directing that story to someone in the group for whom you sensed it was relevant?"

"No."

"Were there several of us that you felt needed to examine something illustrated in the story?"

"No."

"Were you hoping to fixate our attention as an indirect induction?"

"No."

"Well, was it a metaphor meant to convey something at unconscious levels?"

"No."

"Well, then, why did you tell the story?"

Erickson smiled. "I just thought it was an interesting story about good therapy."

That night I dream about long branches, a swamp, and two women talking about "pokeweed" — the plant with juicy berries that are used for making purple dye. There is a couch made of it. It is a hot, gulf night, heavy with an incipient storm. The couch is made of the same purple cloth as Erickson's clothes. The women are talking about being "three legged." There are swamp shadows, all about us, a hot storm coming.

I wake up at three or so burning with the dry Arizona

air. I want a drink of water — badly — but not wanting it enough to go to the trouble of getting up, I lie there, with my mouth like chambray, thinking about water, and the hot desert, and storms: pokeweed, three-legged women.

At Erickson's the next day, Cathy and Lorna get me into the hot seat next to him. He is brought into the room, and before he can begin speaking, we pause for the ritual ceremony of the hooking of the recorders: a spider's web of microphones and wires from cassette machines are attached to his purple robe. Most of the participants want to be sure that Erickson, and his words, don't escape them, forever. And recorders popping to a halt throughout the day don't seem to bother the master — just me.

We have something even more irksome than noisy tape recorders: a lady psychologist from New York. She is quite sizeable, as is her voice. Like the rest of us, she can't understand half of what Erickson is saying, but instead of viewing this as The Breaks when you are around the master, she keeps interrupting him with "I didn't catch that," or "Whudja say, Doctor Erickson?" or "He put it up against her *what*?"

Erickson overlooks her strident interruptions for about an hour — he is remarkably patient; but then after she says, "I didn't hear, Doctor, they looked up into her *what*?" yet again — he gives *her* the *what*: He looks directly at her, closes his eyes, and, by my troth! — she falls back on the couch in a deep trance, staying there (where she well belongs) for a half hour or so. Then, as she bestirs herself, shaking her head and blinking, he looks at her wide-eyed again, closes his eyes, and again she falls back in a swoon where, I would guess, her hearing, insight, and peacefulness are considerably improved.

Erickson, as usual, asks for questions, and I say, "Yes, how do you put someone in a trance who doesn't want to go into a trance, and, number two, how do you treat headaches?" I tell him about the migraines I've had for the past thirty years.

He starts another series of stories: about a guy in the Wisconsin prison system who was a five-time loser; and then one about Sam, the alcoholic, who needed a place to stay, and so Erickson said he could stay in his backyard but he would have to give up his boots. The stories go on all day, and watching him, I think about how amazing he is. He has people from all over the world vying to spend a day with him. He is the acknowledged master of Reframing and Hypnotherapy. Under most circumstances, this old man would be put away in some home for the aged and crippled, but he has a force that has carried him on his own for seventy-five years, and he is still going strong: they say he only recently gave up his Sunday sessions. "I've been living on borrowed time for forty-five years," he's fond of saying, "and I don't have to pay it back."

He has carved out a therapy system all by himself, from himself, and has taught himself to work with all types: depressives, manic-depressives, schizophrenics, juvenile delinquents, suicides, and families (he is considered to be one of the earliest, and most original, practitioners of Family Therapy). He has mastered some of the most diverse methods of establishing rapport with patients. He has found, for one, that he could work with autistics by breathing in rhythm with them. He connects with patients by speaking their language. Someone will say things like "How does that grab you?" or "It was a real gut-wrenching experience." He has learned to spot this type of individual, and respond in kind: "Can you get a handle on what I'm saying?"

He learned to communicate with patients in what they call "the back wards" of mental hospitals by *accepting* their antisocial behaviors, and then redesigning them — on their terms — so that the cycle of depression, lunacy, or simple non-communication could be broken. He is one of the few to communicate successfully with schizophrenics who speak word salad (what Jung called "klang" speech). His method is to repeat the gibberish back to the patient *changing only the vowels*. It is said that after awhile patients can't stand it anymore, and will do anything to shut him up — even by putting an end to their psychotic behavior patterns. There's only room for one in that crowded hotel of delusion.

At 2:45 he turns to me, and says, "Do you understand?"

"I don't know," I say.

"When did you know that you were going to ask me those two questions?"

"This morning, in the hotel, about ten."

"When did *I* know you were going to ask me those two questions?"

"I don't know," I say.

"When I saw you sitting in that chair," he says. "Close your eyes," he says. He makes a ring of thumb and forefinger with his one good hand, puts it about my wrist, raises my arm, and I am gone.

Now don't ask me what happened. I wasn't there, remember? I do recall a voice coming at me, and my hand moving up towards my face, stopping when it got to the halfway mark. I remember him whispering to me about pain, about taking a cool drink, and lying out in the sun. Then I hear him talk about "the devil looking over your shoulder," and have a powerful vision of a big fat gargoyle from some medieval French cathedral — a monster all lips and tongue, hovering there in front of my face, looking right at me.

When I come to, he and all the others are back in his office. He's signing their books and asking each lady for a kiss on the cheek. I stagger up, go to the bathroom for some more Aim, and there, right next to the sink, is a black spider. I turn on the light; I look closely and sure enough, there are those red triangles on the spider's belly or abdomen or whatever you call it. I go out to his office and announce, "There's a black widow spider in the bathroom and I was scared he was going to bite me." Lorna corrects me: "You thought *she* was going to bite you." Erickson goes on signing books.

Cathy, Lorna and I fly back to California that night. The next morning I developed the most wretching pain in my back, right under the shoulder blade. It stays there a full month. I can scarcely get out of bed for the first week. It wakes me at night, makes my days a misery.

I didn't have any headaches, though — for the first time in thirty years, I didn't have a single headache. Not for a full month. "How in God's name did he do that?" I wondered. "What did he say to me when he had me in that trance?"

He never gave me the opportunity to come back and question him about it. The old pokeweed son of a bitch died a year or so later, a week before we were to go back for another visit.

CHAPTER 14

Neurosis seems to be a human privilege.

— Sigmund Freud
Moses and Monotheism

The last night of the conference, I repair to the Hyatt Regency watering hole. I have become autistic from psychodynamic overload, coupled with traces of anxiety (will I ever get out of Phoenix?), alienation (there are too many psychotherapists in the world), displacement (I need another drink), and psychotaxis depression (if I hear one more schizophrenia success story, I'll cry.)

Despite my burgeoning catalepsy, I attract the attention of a wiry counselor from the eastern shore of Maryland by the name of Lisa. She is a helper, another that I define as a Trench Worker. She tells of alcoholics, the wife- and child-abusers, the lonely and the depressed, all the terminal cases that she sees in the course of a week. "The trouble with this conference," she says, "is that they tell you techniques for dealing with stuck families, or wife beaters, or alcoholic, violent fathers — but they don't tell you how to deal with all of these in the same family: Where do you begin?"

Like most people in the helping profession, Lisa is in there trying to *help*. She gets a crummy salary, miserable working conditions, and terrible bosses. Every time there is a budget cut in Maryland social services, it is her department that is affected. She does what she can — as best she is able — to bring some kind of solace to the hundreds of clients in her all-too-large service area. She is a social worker because she cares for the job. Like most of her peers in the profession, she is conscientious, thoughtful, and wise beyond her years. She does some counseling on her own.

"What do you do for a living?" she asks me.

"I'm a taxidermist," I tell her.

"Really?" she says. "How interesting. Why are you attending this conference?" she says.

"Actually I'm at the meeting next door," I tell her, "The AASA — the Ataxic Animal Stuffers of America. We just happen to be here at the same time as — what do they call your group?"

"What do you do for a living?" she asks.

"Actually, I was just joking. All that about me being a taxidermist. I'm a reporter — press and radio. I'm here covering your conference," I say. "I just said all that about taxidermy because I'm basically shy."

"Hm," she says. "You say you're shy. What do you mean?"

"It might have something to do with the fact that my father was a taxidermist, and my mother was into ichthyology. I was always afraid that they were going to stuff me."

"You say your father was a taxidermist?" she says.

"No, I'm just being silly. Actually my father was a

lawyer who divorced my mother and married his job. And my mother divorced her children and adopted stocks and bonds."

"What makes you think you are shy?" she says.

Those therapists! They never really stop practicing their craft, do they? Do surgeons come home and cut up their children? Do plumbers come home and take the hot water heater apart? Do attorneys come home and cross-examine their wives?

"I never know what to say to people," I say, "so I just shut up."

"Can you think back to the time in your life when you first felt that way? I mean, can you shut your eyes right now and go back to where you first felt this?" Lisa is the compleat therapist, and I suppose she'd have to be fairly enthusiastic about her chosen profession to stay in it for thirty years and stay alert and alive, much less go to the trouble of psychoanalysing me in the Fern Room of the Hyatt Regency. I can tell by her determination that she is a full time mind-worker.

"I don't have to shut my eyes," I tell her: "I already know." I haven't been on the receiving end of the Shrink Biz all these years for nothing. I tell her a few of my secrets. Lisa and I embark on a bit of Friday evening barroom Psychotherapeutic Sunday Afternoon Touch Football. She's been a "helper" for as long as I have been a "client." We both know the rules of our respective trades, and we are both good at them. This brief interchange hints at what she and I do in our outside, non-conference world, a give-and-take, leading us together into the next stage of our lives, whatever that might be.

Murray Bowen, in his wisdom, says there have been therapists around for centuries, perhaps for as long as people have been speaking with more than guttural grunts and cries. Somewhere, five thousand years ago, in Chaldea, at the edge of the Euphrates, there must have been a good, nonjudgmental, non-critical, supportive listener. In India, at the time of the birth of the Masters, there was another kind of Master, wasn't there? — an early Master of the Masters, not saying "No," or "What you are thinking is wrong," or "You have sinned" — but, rather, giving forth with an understanding phrase: "It may be best not to judge others — or even yourself," he might have said. "The dreams," he would say: "They are hard to give up, aren't they? Harder, even, perhaps, than giving up the anger . . . "

Our seer from the past, living in a simple place, with whitewashed walls, two chairs, a bottle of wine, a table — perhaps even a golden bird to turn its head, to watch what is transpiring with unblinking, bright eyes. "Of course," the sage says, "Of course it hurts. It goes around, going around, again and again. You aren't sure what you have lost," he says, "that may be the pain of it."

I can see the two of them now, see them seated at the edge of the dusty square, or in the darkness at the side of the cathedral; along the great medieval wall, next to the quiet stream. A man listens patiently to a tale of suffering that we, as humans, seem to be capable of inflicting on ourselves, and on others. The quiet listener nods, making it easy to speak, to ease out the hurt — the gulph of pain, the birthing of agony. He is the midwife of a freedom — giving us the chance to escape what they used to call "the agenbite of inwit."

Et semel emmisum volat irrevocabile verbum. Once the words take flight into the void, they need not return. Words carry the buzzard out, the buzzard that has been pecking so viciously at the soul for so long. The wound that we think can never be healed is, slowly, despite ourselves, ameliorated. It never goes away, entirely — but it does get turned. It is like a great flawed jewel. There are other angles from which we can view it, making it not so unendurable. The words pass, the pain gets parted a bit; the soul comes to feel lighter, raised out of the dark.

Bowen is right. We've been talking ourselves out of the worst of agon for æons, telling secrets to the one who understands, who cares, who will not judge. The feelings we have nursed are not futile, and they certainly are not wrong — but they can be transcended. The yielding in itself may cause anguish. It is part of the knowledge that we are surrendering — but it is also the knowledge that we are surrendering to ourselves. That knowledge is magic. Painful it is, but, at the same time, magic.

A non-judgmental hearer, there to ease us out of the midnight of feelings, ease us into freedom, with our own words. It *is* magic. Perhaps as special as the magic they say grew from the visions of Lourdes.

■ ■ ■

Q. Dr. Laing, I'd like to ask you about Dr. Whitaker's thought about giving up working with individual patients?

Whitaker. I have, yeah. I think it's ridiculous. I think it's bilateral. I'll tell you what I think it is.

Laing. Go on.

Whitaker. Is it all right if I do?

Laing. Sure.

Whitaker. I think individual therapy is transgenerational, psychological incest.

Laing. Ya. That sounds lovely.

Whitaker. Like a one-parent family. There's no such

thing as a one-parent family yet. I don't know what's gonna happen if the women can clone themselves. We're gonna be in trouble.

Q. I mean, Ronny, you work mostly with individuals. As far as I know, you do very little of any group work or family work.

Whitaker. I didn't say I was *against* incest, don't misunderstand me.

Laing. Incest is all right as long as you keep it in the family.

Whitaker. Vice is nice, but incest is best. The angel of God.

Laing. I still see people individually. I haven't developed the same degree of disillusionment out of my own practice of seeing people individually as Carl has. I've got a lot of reservations about the whole practice of psychotherapy as well. But I haven't got to the end of the line of practicing psychotherapy. I think there's always going to be a place in life where one person talks to another person about problems, in private, and in confidence. I certainly would like to feel I had the opportunity to go along and consult someone alone about my relationships with other people. I would like that opening to still be there.

Whitaker. Oh ya — I was going to say that. If I had that kind of thing, I would *love* to go and talk to Ronny by myself.

FIN

Comments on the Interview with Christy

I shall confine my comments to the transcript of the thirty minute conversation with Christy, a "street person" from Phoenix. She had a DSM-III† diagnosis of, as I recall, deluded, hallucinated, inadequately groomed, treatment-resistant schizophrenic mental disorder.

I wanted to converse, to turn things around together, with a real, card-carrying "schizophrenic." I specified that I required a person to interview *who was not on medication* so, despite scouring around for something like a 100 mile radius, the organizers could find no such person until Christy turned up. She was discovered the night before, I believe.

The organizers at the Milton Erickson Institute probably withheld their blessing to the publication of this interview because they felt that the transcript could not convey the main point. I agree. The main point is in the rhythm, the tempo — the timbre and pitch of the words that are in the *paralinguistics*. There is between Christy and me, a music of words. There are, as well, *kinesics* — concerted movements involving arm, hand, finger, leg, the positions of our bodies in the chairs, set at 90 degrees to each other.

†*Diagnostic and Statistical Manual of Mental Disorders* of the American Psychiatric Association; Third Edition — 1980.

The paralinguistics and kinesics — the *music* and the *dance* — were much emphasized by Milton Erickson in his teachings, but most "professionals" are amazingly impervious to all that. It is a question of the complete opera, with singers, costumes, sets, backdrops, and orchestra, versus the mere libretto. You are publishing the libretto (the verbal content) without the music (the pitch, timbre, rhythm, tempo, the paralinguistics) and without the choreography (two symmetrical chairs placed precisely as intended), and the ballet (*kinesics*).

The point is that the *rapport* which seemed to so many so "mysterious," "mystifying," or "mystical" (the "love" to which Salvador Minuchin referred in his remarks) is there on video for all to see and to analyze in detail. There is a lot of technique there. Many people like Christy do not connect with "content" alone, if the sound and movements of the therapist are, in effect, *autistic*. That is, if the therapist in his/her presence as manifested through sight and sound is effectively selectively inattentive to 99 percent of the sight and sound of the patient/client.

— *R. D. Laing*
Going, Austria
October 1988

Presentation of R. D. Laing At the Evolution of Psychotherapy Conference December 13, 1985

[The initial part of the presentation takes place in a booth separated by curtains from the conference hall and the conference-goers. R. D. Laing and the subject, Christy, can hear the audience but cannot see them. The audience can see and hear Christy and Laing by means of video cameras and large screens set in the auditorium.]

Dr. Laing. I can't hear you.
Christy. You can't hear me?
Dr. Laing. I can hear you now, yes.
Christy. . . . says when you try to torture him he's gonna get . . . uh . . . a parachute and bail out.
Dr. Laing. Ah . . . to the nether regions. [Laughing]
Christy. Huh?
Dr. Laing. To the upper regions.
Christy. To the what?
Dr. Laing. To the nether or upper regions. Anyway you aren't . . . I don't know anything about you at all. And I don't know what to ask you about yourself, you know. What

would you feel is appropriate to say under the circumstances?

Christy. I don't know. [Laughs]

Dr. Laing. Is there anything that, uh . . . do you feel that your situation is okay for you just now, or — you say, you tell me, coming over, that you're taking some *nox vomica* to calm your system.

Christy. And to sharpen my stupid wits.

Dr. Laing. Ya. What is it that's creating the static in your system? The stopping in your system?

Christy. Oh, well, I think my brain don't work right.

Dr. Laing. In what way?

Christy. Oh let me see, well I get, I get the *nox vomica* doesn't treat this per se . . . I'm getting another remedy for that problem. I get things turned around. I get opposites confused. I get, when I write, I get my letters confused, I get words confused. The end. And . . . either I tend to be paranoid, or they really are after me — I don't know which.

Dr. Laing. Uh . . . So you're not sure whether you're confused about that or not?

Christy. About what?

Dr. Laing. About whether they really are after you or not.

Christy. Oh, he sounds like it. [Pointing at cameraman]

Dr. Laing. What, him?

Christy. Oh, ya. [Laugh together]

Dr. Laing. You might be after me for all I know.

Christy. Well I'm just trying to help you guys get some sense into your brains. I don't know if it's worth it though, you know? I had a guru for a long time who said there isn't any sense in it, what you gotta do to, to be able to perceive reality is attain a level of consciousness which he offered, which I never attained, which is — he said — beyond the mind. It's completely above the mind.

Dr. Laing. What sort of guru is this character?
Christy. This is, this is guru Maharaji.
Dr. Laing. Ah, well, what do you take him to mean by that? Beyond the mind, uh . . . above the mind?
Christy. Well whatever it is I couldn't imagine with my mind, because it's beyond the mind. I suppose it's some sort of . . . I suppose it involves a universal being, conscious of the Universal Consciousness. You know, everybody is subconsciously aware of everybody else's mind. Well, you know that. I've seen that. I've seen you read my mind.
Dr. Laing. I don't see how you can be conscious of the Universal Mind. The Universal Mind's conscious of you. But you're not conscious of it.
Christy. I . . . uh . . . Well.
Dr. Laing. Y' know.
Christy. Maybe so, maybe out of my bitterness I just say "Well, the Universal Mind doesn't know anything." [Laughing] Maybe I say that because I look around and I don't see any superior intelligence taking care of anything. [Pause]
Dr. Laing. How would you expect to see a . . . you mean that all the pain and suffering, stupidity, and confusion in the world . . . how can there be a Universal Mind, if a Universal Mind allows that sort of stuff to go on?
Christy. Ya. Especially stupidity.
Dr. Laing. Ah . . . maybe the, either the, either the Universal Mind is stupid itself, or it's mad itself, or it doesn't exist.
Christy. Oh it exists. It might be the sum total of the human minds, but it exists.
Dr. Laing. Well are you trying to . . . well, I mean I've spent a lot of time trying to work out how that can be the case. If it is the case. But I haven't found any answer to that

myself. But I still put a coat and tie on under the circumstances. Why not? [Laughs]

Christy. Ya . . . I asked him why he didn't kill himself, he said he's not ready yet.

Dr. Laing. Uh huh.

Christy. Well, I guess if you're dead you'll blow any chance of doing anything good, huh?

Dr. Laing. This time 'round.

Christy. Huh?

Dr. Laing. This time 'round, anyway. [Pause] If we were just sitting here without these uh . . . cameras on and these microphones, I wouldn't say anything just now, but I feel impelled to make an effort to keep talking for the sake of people who are listening to it. Maybe I shouldn't bother.

Christy. Are people listening to this?

Dr. Laing. Ya . . . a whole lot of people are listening. That's part of the . . .

Christy. Nobody told me that the camera was on.

Dr. Laing. The camera, that guy as far as I know has got the camera on us just now. And there are a whole lot of people listening to it.

Christy. Geez, I wouldn't have talked about that stuff if I'd of known it was on.

Dr. Laing. It doesn't matter. [Laughs] How long have you been in Phoenix then?

Christy. A year and a half.

Dr. Laing. And what brought you to Phoenix?

Christy. I was trying to escape the conspiracy, and it didn't work.

Dr. Laing. What conspiracy?

Christy. Well if there is one I suppose you're a conspirator so you know already. If there isn't, I guess I just imagined it.

Dr. Laing. Well, whether or not I'm a conspirator and

whether or not you're imagining it, are you prepared to give me your account of what that conspiracy is?

Christy. As much as I can figure out, yeah.

Dr. Laing. Well go ahead.

Christy. Well, I think the conspiracy doesn't exist, so I just don't think about it. If I don't think about it it's not there too much. But then people like Peter, people like Dr. Stumph, you know they tend to like make me believe in it again. So, I try to avoid those people. I'm not even gonna talk to you any more. No, he's alright when he's talking about the job.

Dr. Laing. Is it a benign conspiracy or a malign conspiracy?

Christy. Huh?

Dr. Laing. Is it a conspiracy for good or for evil?

Christy. Well . . . oh heck if I know. But if anybody messes with me like that, I don't care. You know what I figure is, you see, the mind creates a whole lot of things . . . you know. I mean I see mine as really powerful. And people, subconsciously, their minds always enter it. They do, I've seen that, you know. And people see what they expect to see. So it just stands to reason if I believe in a conspiracy, people are going to act like conspirators.

Dr. Laing. Ya . . . so far okay.

Christy. Ya, but I told Dr. Stumph . . . he walked into the room just as I was saying something negative about doctors but he didn't know that he heard it.

Dr. Laing. Well who walked into the room . . . Peter?

Christy. Huh?

Dr. Laing. Who walked into the room just as you were saying something negative?

Christy. Dr. Stumph.

Dr. Laing. Ah.

Christy. But I don't know — maybe I expected him to walk

in when I was saying something negative about doctors. I mean they try.

Dr. Laing. Well, that sort of thing is happening all the time. I mean I don't see what you're making a special point of that about.

Christy. What do you mean?

Dr. Laing. I don't see why you are making a special point of telling me that just now since that sort of thing as you know I know, and I know you know, happens all the time anyway.

Christy. Ya, well — 'cause they're watching us.

Dr. Laing. Well, ya, alright . . . we better stop that. [Laughs] I mean this whole set-up is an enormous conspiracy, and you're right in the heart of the conspiracy just now.

Christy. Oh.

Dr. Laing. So you haven't . . . if you came to Phoenix to get away from the conspiracy, you haven't done very well.

Christy. What do you mean?

Dr. Laing. Well you're sitting here in this situation.

Christy. You mean the conference is a conspiracy?

Dr. Laing. Ya, of course.

Christy. What kind of a conspiracy?

Dr. Laing. Well I've got a plane booked to get to Boston Sunday, so I'm not going to say what sort of conspiracy it is because I want to go on that plane, you know, and get out of here as far as I'm concerned. No, I think it's quite a benign conspiracy. It's certainly a very concerted deep plan. And it involves . . . it's much wider than the number of people that are actually here. 7,000 people have flown in and that's a sort of minor conspiracy in terms of the galaxy, but it's quite a bit of a conspiracy.

Christy. Well how do you know about it? What do you know about it?

Dr. Laing. Well I guess . . . I think the Universal Mind has

been asleep a bit, as far as this planet goes. I mean in this galaxy, and this planet. It's uh . . . itching a bit. And it's sort of waking up a bit, sort of to do something about it.
Christy. It is capable of doing anything.
Dr. Laing. Ah, oh, well Jesus Christ has got no other hands but ours.
Christy. Oh.
Dr. Laing. I mean it's only capable of doing what we do. I mean as far as we're concerned.
Christy. Are you a Christian?
Dr. Laing. Well that depends on who I'm talking to.
Christy. Well . . . just tell me.
Dr. Laing. Oh, if I'm talking to you? Well I'm not sure what I should say about that. I'm a Christian in the sense that Jesus Christ wasn't crucified between two candlesticks in a cathedral. He was crucified in the town garbage heap between two thieves. In that sense I'm a Christian.
Christy. You're a what?
Dr. Laing. What?
Christy. I didn't hear your last word.
Dr. Laing. In that sense I'm a Christian. But I mean in another sense, in another sense I mean I wouldn't admit to being a Christian in most Christian company. Why? Are you a Christian?
Christy. Hell no.
Dr. Laing. Huh?
Christy. I don't think so. I think God doesn't know what he's doing, so who knows, maybe Jesus had a mental problem, you know?
Dr. Laing. Well . . . maybe he didn't have time to mature. They got him too young.
Christy. Ya, or maybe . . . I was talking to my friend about this the other day. I told him I don't believe in God. He says

he believes in many gods and they eat their disciples after they die.

Dr. Laing. Oh?

Christy. So maybe that's what Jesus does?

Dr. Laing. Well, worse things could happen than if when I die I was eaten up by Jesus. Sounds quite a bit Gospel, doesn't it?

Christy. You think it would be okay? Well I thought it might be better than getting eaten by the devil.

Dr. Laing. It might be indeed.

Christy. But then it might be better not to get eaten at all.

Dr. Laing. Well I don't think you can help that.

Christy. Excuse me?

Dr. Laing. I don't think you can help it. We're either . . . we're either in the bowels of hell or in the bowels of heaven. Or both at one time.

Christy. The what?

Dr. Laing. The bowels.

Christy. Oh, ya. Well I think that's awfully mean. But then that's just what my friend says. It doesn't mean it's true.

Dr. Laing. Do you think it's fair? You say it's awfully mean.

Christy. I think it's awfully mean that humans are at the consciousness we're at. We're just half-way some place. We're intelligent, but we're not intelligent enough. At least I haven't figured anything out, have you? You're older.

Dr. Laing. What difference does that make?

Christy. Well you've had more time. Have you figured anything out?

Dr. Laing. You don't get any wiser when you get older.

Christy. See. [Audience laughs]

Dr. Laing. Well — *that* got a laugh. [Both laugh] What about your Mom and Dad and that sort of thing. What sort of, are they alive?

Christy. Who . . . my parents?
Dr. Laing. Yeah.
Christy. Ya.
Dr. Laing. What sort of chap was your father?
Christy. Oh, well — he's a Christian preacher.
Dr. Laing. Oh, I didn't know.
Christy. Yeah, my parents are very religious. At least they say they are.
Dr. Laing. Well . . . you're very religious.
Christy. You know what my . . . ya, I guess I am.
Dr. Laing. Oh, it's not meant as an insult.
Christy. And my parents are currently running a shelter up in Michigan.
Dr. Laing. What?
Christy. They are running a shelter.
Dr. Laing. Uh-huh.
Christy. Yes.
Dr. Laing. Where was that?
Christy. Flint.
Dr. Laing. How do they feel about you?
Christy. I don't know. I don't know. I wrote them, I don't know. I wrote them a letter and asked them and . . . I haven't picked it up in the mail yet, I asked them if it was okay for me to send a Christmas present. That's . . . I don't know.
Dr. Laing. No reply?
Christy. I haven't been to the post office yet to pick it up. That's if they did reply. They probably did.
Dr. Laing. Do you expect them to send you a Christmas present?
Christy. Oh God, I don't know. Let's see I was . . . I had some Christmas gifts so I thought I'd send them some. 'Cause I was making crafts for Christmas.

Dr. Laing. Because you were making?

Christy. Crafts.

Dr. Laing. Crafts? Uh huh. I would never have thought of writing my parents and asking them if it was okay for me to send them a present for Christmas. I mean, why wouldn't it be okay?

Christy. Well, because maybe they hate me after all I . . . after being an unfaithful daughter.

Dr. Laing. Unfaithful to whom? Them?

Christy. Yes, I haven't visited them in years.

Dr. Laing. Uh huh.

Christy. And in fact I don't communicate well with them, either. But, you see, I have my own life to live. You know, I hope they understand that. But maybe they don't.

Dr. Laing. Well, if you're faithful to the Lord Jesus Christ, how can you be unfaithful to your father? Well, I mean, he said that, didn't he? "Unless you hate your father and mother — and follow me — you can't be a disciple."

Christy. Ya.

Dr. Laing. What does your father make of that?

Christy. Well, probably that, uh . . . well this current Christian emphasis on family is uh . . . is against the teachings of Jesus. You know the modern Christian emphasis on families.

Dr. Laing. Ya, I guess. I mean I don't . . . do you know that passage where Jesus . . . I always said I thought there was something wrong with that translation. It said unless you hate your father and mother the prophecy said you cannot be my disciple. In the English version, anyway. I think it means unless you prefer me to your father and mother.

Christy. I don't recall that it said hate. It's something like deny.

Dr. Laing. Ya, I . . . asked a guy, an Aramaic scholar about this, but he said he thought it meant "unless you are happily indifferent to them."

Christy. That makes a lot of sense.

Dr. Laing. Ya, call his bluff.

Christy. Because if you're not happily indifferent to your parents they're gonna be on your case all your life.

Dr. Laing. That's right. [Pause] I have to go back now. I'm gonna get up on stage and talk.

Christy. Okay.

Dr. Laing. Alright?

Christy. Okay.

Dr. Laing. Alright, I'll see you later.

Christy. Okay. Hey can I come out?

Dr. Laing. Want to come out?

Christy. To see what you say, yeah.

[They leave the room and come up and sit at the dais.]

Bill McCloud. Perhaps I could ask if any of the panel would like to make a comment before we go for questions and answers from . . . and comments from the audience?

Q. [To Christy.] How was that for you now that you've seen that there is a large group of people here? Thank you for your graciousness in being here, by the way.

Christy. Oh [Moving closer to the microphone. Audience applauds] . . . They're very nice to clap, they're very nice to clap for us.

Q. [Same person] It's an acknowledgement of your courage. Thank you.

Bill McCloud. Alright . . . so we'll take questions from the audience, if anybody would like to come up and address a question to a member of the panel.

Dr. Laing. Do you want to take an interval? Do you want to take a stretch? No.

Bill McCloud. Here is a question here.

Q. Well I'm only getting up because no one else did. And I want to tell you that my impression was that our young lady is extremely bright. And I'd like you to note from my point of view that one of the reasons I'm at this conference is to answer some of the questions about life that you're looking at through your eyes. And appreciate your being up there.

Bill McCloud. Thank you. Yes?

Q. I was wondering what you thought really went on therapeutically in that interview?

Bill McCloud. You're addressing that to Dr. Laing?

Q. Yes.

Dr. Laing. What do you think went on therapeutically?

Q. [Same person] I'm mystified, to tell you the truth. So maybe you could explain it to me.

Dr. Laing. If you're mystified, I can't explain it to you.

Q. [Same person] Did anything go on?

Bill McCloud. There's an observation perhaps you could make as to who's up on the platform which might partly answer your question. [Applause] Yes?

Q. A couple of days ago, Dr. Laing, you spoke about creating a kind of transpersonal reality, or not creating, but stepping into something that is a shared reality between you and the person you're working with. And that spoke to me very deeply, and I was really interested in hearing from the young lady that you've been interviewing with, and also from you, about the experience of that, that moving into that place. You, and I'm speaking to you, the young woman . . . mentioned some feeling of Dr. Laing having read your mind earlier, and I'd like to hear anything you have to say about that experience? Either as something . . . as his stepping into your . . . your head or the two of you being in some kind of shared reality.

Dr. Laing. [After consulting with Christy]. Neither of us

knows how to answer that question. But all of us have put in a few words to this. And tell me if I'm right or wrong [Looking at Christy]. It's with the greatest reservations that I think one can talk about transpersonal reality. It is certainly non-verbal. And it is fundamentally, essentially, impossible to express in the content of words. It is possible to convey it, however, more in the . . . through words, through . . . in the music of words, in the manner of words. And in the other ways in which I was trying to explain two days ago. We communicate with each other interpersonally. If that realization is present of the transpersonal field, then nothing needs to be said between those people who are aware of that transpersonal field. When one tries to explain one's awareness of that transpersonal field to people who are not aware of it — and I know that in this company there are a lot of you who are aware of it — and many of you who are not aware of it. Now, to those of you who are aware of it, you know how difficult it is to talk about. And to those of you who are not aware of it, I would say this. Don't be too impatient; don't — because you don't understand it, because you are mystified — don't get angry. Something is happening. Something is happening. Something is happening between us in this hall at this very moment. You can't express it in words. There is a conspiracy, there is a divine conspiracy which has brought us together. There is a divine conspiracy as well as a conspiracy of the devil. I'm not going to go on and say any more about that just now, but as I tried to say before, it makes all the difference if there is a sense of communion which is unspoken. It doesn't have to be said. It shouldn't actually be spoken about any more than it sometimes needs to be. Out of which interpersonal communication occurs and links up with the intrapersonal. If that is there, it makes all the difference. If that is absent, it's sort of going at it like this, making interpretations, trying to understand, trying to do psychotherapy, it's the same — whether it's behavioral therapy, psychotherapy, psychoanalytic therapy, or whatnot etc. etc. It will come to nothing. It doesn't . . . it doesn't get anywhere with those people, those people who find it very difficult to live in the world of the interpersonal and the intrapersonal and can see how stupid it all is, how ugly it all is, how inexpressably confused it all is, and yet are just regarded as crazy and mad for realizing that, and are either locked up, or run away.

Q. [Man]. Speaking about conspiracy, I'd like to ask the members of the panel how this young woman came to be interviewed in front of hundreds or thousands of us today without knowing that this was the case?

Christy. I knew it. I knew it was the case.

Dr. Laing. She knew it was the case. She didn't know that the camera started running.

Q. I see.

Dr. Laing. That's all, she knew about it, absolutely, right? You knew it was the case.

Christy. Ya, I knew you guys were watching me. [Touches Laing's shoulder]

Q. [Same person] You knew we were watching?

Christy. I didn't know when they started the cameras.

Q. [Same person] I got it. I got it. Thank you.

Bill McCloud. Yes.

Q. [Man]. It seems to me that what seems to be happening is that a vacuum has been created. It reminds me of a professor friend of mine who said "I feel, I feel, I don't know what I feel, but oh how I feel." And what I'm wondering is, that vacuum allows people in the medical profession to bring zombies to us and we have to work with them. And the vacuum doesn't really, uh . . . give to me, at least, a feeling of understanding, and when you refuse to understand, refuse . . . it sounds sort of nirvanish. And although I'm not against that, I think that some kind of clearer explanation, clearer understanding should be given, so we know what we're doing. And when you avoid those things, you're breaking down the whole therapeutic process, it would seem to me. Enlightenment does not come just by remaining silent . . . although that's a nice feeling.

Dr. Laing. This young lady sitting beside me is supposed to be an absolute paranoid schizophrenic on medication. She's sitting here just now perfectly *compos mentus*, perfectly clear, facing this most intimidating situation from this stage, not exhibiting any symptoms of schizophrenic disorder. If you knew of any medication that could do that in twenty minutes, from there to here, would you say you wouldn't give that to a patient? You would have to spend the rest of your life being a biochemist to understand what the chemical affects of that sort of thing is supposed to be in the central nervous system. [Intensely] So you don't know anything about this sort of process. Have the humility to admit that, and keep your place. Instead of the arrogance that you seem to have, to think that you . . . because you don't know something . . . that there's something the matter with those people who do. [Applause.]

Q. [Same person] No, I didn't say that I don't. I have a mind that can understand, I'm sure you do. And I don't think we should call each other names, and say "arrogance." I think there is more arrogance in silence, sometimes, than there is in expressing wisdom, if somebody has it. If there is wisdom give it to us. But don't let us feel as though there's some kind of a mystical communion going on when there isn't. And to call . . .

Dr. Laing. There is. There is, that's the point. There certainly is. But, see . . . you say when there's some kind of mystical communion going on when there isn't.

Q. [Same person] Well again it's "I feel" — "I feel."

Dr. Laing. [Loudly] Ya, "I feel," "I feel," "I feel" — who's talking about I feel?

Q. [Same person] "I don't know what I feel, but, oh, how I feel it!"

Dr. Laing. Well I do know! And you don't know! And I'm saying that it is not verbal. And it can't be put into words. And because you can't understand it, obviously, you say — "ha, ha, ha, some sort of mystical communion going on."

Q. [Same person] But there are people who have claimed to see the devil. There are people who have claimed all kinds of things.

Dr. Laing. Give someone else a chance at the microphone!

Q. [Same person] If it . . . if it bothers you I can quit.

Dr. Laing. [Loudly] It bothers me!

Bill McCloud. Thank you.

Q. Thank you. Since we have the doctors on the panel up there, I wonder if they will be willing to take this opportunity to talk about their own struggles with medicating the folks at CHAPS. I was over there last night and met them and I'm sure that they do struggle with this. And those of us who work in a system struggle very much with the issue of medication, particularly around relief of pain, as opposed to control of behavior. I'd just like to hear the doctors and other members of the panel address that directly.

Bill McCloud. Dr. Stumph?

Dr. Stumph. Thank you. That has been quite an issue within our program. Briefly our program CHAPS, County

Homeless Alternative Psychiatric Services, is a store-front Bowery area clinic. We're down there in between the homeless shelter and the euphemistically labeled Open Air Park, and the plasma center. Our mandate, or what we're paid to do, is to locate homeless people who have been diagnosed chronically mentally ill. And of course those that pay us have a strict set of criteria as to what's to be considered chronically mentally ill, and what is not. We're a voluntary program and essentially we're a place for people to come when they have nowhere else to go. People are welcome to show up, have a sandwich, have a cup of coffee, watch the television, talk with people. One of our first goals is to find folks a decent place to live, make sure that they have somewhere they can get their three square meals a day, and address other concrete concerns, on-going medical problems that need to be treated. Often times we find just by removing people from the street environment and placing them somewhere stable, or helping them find somewhere stable to live, we see tremendous gains in terms of reduction of psychosis, diminution of symptoms, and people just generally get along much better. For example, Christy, when I had first seen her — do you mind me saying — it was back in the summer I saw her twice at the CHAPS center, where she had come in. I really can't say why the motivation . . . I imagine she had heard about us some from other people around. Is that right? How come you came to CHAPS, Christy — the first time? Had you heard about us? You were referred? Oh . . . one of the guys at the shelter then saw her and said that she might want to drop by. We saw her once or twice, sat and talked. And then I didn't see her again until last night when she fortuitously showed up. I would posit, since when I saw Christy in the summer — and she was doing quite poorly by my criteria in that she exhibited loose association, prominent delusions, was visibly hallucinating, and was disoriented. Now of course she's much better. But I would posit that a great deal of that gain is not due so much to any other factor than that she now has a stable place to live. [Christy shakes her head, and moves to mike. Audience laughs. Dr. Stumph continues] I think one of the national shames within our society is that right here within our city while we're sitting comfortably, there are over a thousand mentally-ill persons who slept last night on the streets.

Bill McCloud. You can't see it Michael, but there's disagreement from this end of the table.

Christy. No, that's not why I'm doing that.

Dr. Stumph. No, why are you doing that?

Christy. I explained, I explained it last night, if you remember.

Dr. Stumph. I do. Would you like to tell them? Go ahead.

Christy. The reason I'm doing better is because I quit putting mental energy into the . . . into the conspiracy. And creating it, to a certain point. But this guy [Points to Laing] says that there is one. And I think that's because you know how to share minds, it's because he knows how to tap into other people's minds. [Looks at Laing] You know on a subtle level — not by just asking questions. Because everybody reads minds. You guys read minds. I tell ya, everybody does. And if you observe, if you look around, you'll notice it. Thank you. And I would like to say something else while I got this. I don't go around like a paranoid schizophrenic all the time. I know how to keep my cool. [Applause] And I think this guy would be a great psychotherapist, because he does that. [Laughter] Because he knows how to tap into other people's . . . where other people's minds are at. You know not by just asking questions and trying to figure things out like some [Nods at Dr. Stumph].

Bill McCloud. Thank you. We have time for a few more questions.

Q. [Woman] Okay, just briefly, I'm having a real difficult time reading the doctor's mind at this point. I still don't feel that he addressed the issue of medication.

Dr. Stumph. You're probably right. I didn't go quite far enough. I do utilize medicines. Again we're a voluntary program. I believe that a modern-day psychiatrist has to be well-versed in all types of therapies. Including medical therapies, analytical therapies, other dynamic therapies, and lastly — social therapies. To do only one type of therapy for all types of patients is inappropriate. Some patients benefit from one approach, other patients benefit from another approach. When I feel patients can benefit from some sort of medication for symptom reduction, then I certainly offer it. We're a voluntary program, nobody takes anything that they don't want to take. But I do use medicines quite extensively.

Q. [Same person] What I was told is that they are very strongly encouraged to take medication. That's what I was told by the social worker at CHAPS. That that is an agenda of the program.

Dr. Stumph. At times, ya. We don't twist people's arms and threaten to throw them out into the street. We provide services to folks whether or not they take medicines. Right. Thank you. In general the folks I see . . . they've been called chronic. Generally, they're going to have some sort of symptoms life-long. I'm much more concerned that they come away with a good experience with their psychiatrist, and grow to trust psychiatrists a bit more, and be able to turn to us when they need to, than I am in momentarily reducing symptoms with medication. However, medications can be literally life-saving . . . when appropriately used.

Q. [Same person] Thank you. I just wonder if there's anyone else on the panel who would like to add to that and I'm going to sit down?

Bill McCloud. Good, thank you.

Q. [Different woman] This is on the lighter side, and it's for Dr. Laing, and his friend on his left. On Tuesday I didn't get an opportunity to ask him, and I have a big need to ask him, if he is indeed conversant with the novelist Doris Lessing? I'm a fan of hers and a fan of his. I didn't get a chance to ask that question. Today, along comes this young woman who has a remarkable resemblance to Doris Lessing, physically . . . I see. And I just want to say that I see that as sort of a synchronistic event. But it is still a question. Did you hear me?

Dr. Laing. Yes, um . . . I've met Doris Lessing, yes. And I've read some of Doris Lessing's work, and of course I very much admire her as a writer, and like her as a person.

Q. [Same person] I felt particularly in *The Four Gated City*, she was influenced by your work. If you remember that book.

Dr. Laing. Well I think she has been. She certainly has said so in writing.

Q. [Same person] Thank you.

Salvador Minuchin. My question goes to Dr. Laing and the young lady. I would like you to tell me . . . all the people here at the same time . . . that how is it for you, young lady — I don't know your name — how is it for you to be here . . . there . . . with us now? And for Dr. Laing, what does that mean to you?

Christy. Well, I hope you guys can learn something.

[Audience laughs]

Bill McCloud. That says it all, thank you.

Salvador Minuchin. Okay, I loved it. I thought it was wonderful. And I think that you should learn something from Ronald. Because I don't think you did. You see, what we have experienced here is a communion of love. What I was observing, and I felt in trance, I felt in love with this young person. And she was able to elicit from Ronald, and so did he from her, that kind of experience, it was experienced at the level not of the words, but there was an element of joining, that was expressed in their hands, in their legs, they were moving exactly in the same place, and I loved it. And I think it's important that you should know that. I am talking to the physician that talks about drugs. Because the drug that existed there is very, very powerful. [Bravos from the audience]

Bill McCloud. Thank you, Dr. Minuchin. One more question, and then we'll leave it at that.

Q. May I ask a point of information, and I think only the young lady can answer this. You've been introduced as one of the homeless, and undoubtedly you have met many others on the street. How many of you if . . . and I don't know if it's fair for me to ask you to speak for others — but how many of you would choose to stay where you are if people would leave you alone? [Pause] I'm asking this because it's somehow disturbing to many others to see somebody without a place. So they want to make a place for them. And what's more they want to make a place for them, for homeless people, altogether, you know, bunched, and I wonder if that's a good thing?

Christy. The worst thing about being on the streets is feeling threatened by other people who, who try to do harm to street people. And it doesn't help a person to feel less like people are out to get 'em either, you know.

Bill McCloud. Thank you.

Dr. Stumph. May I answer that question please before we sign off? I'd like to, because it brings in with the last question about the power of love. I have yet to meet any of our clients on the street that enjoy being there. They're there because circumstances have forced them there. It is quite dangerous, it is quite uncomfortable. No one wants to be there. Most of our clients are unloved. Very few clients are articulate and attractive, like Christy. Our more typical client is visibly disoriented, dressed inappropriately for weather, louse-ridden, angry, hostile, making no sense when he talks. These people are not loved within our society, and I think that gives us something to think about.

Bill McCloud. Good, thank you. If I could, while I was listening to the questioning, I was thinking of some lines of Dr. Laing's poem, "Knots", and the lines which occured to me have a lot of irony in them of course, but they apply to you and me perhaps.

They are playing a game,
They are not playing a game,
How dare you laugh when Christ died for you.

And I saw a lot of laughter and, as Dr. Minuchin said, the contact between the two, I think, was an expression of the playfulness which can occur even when discussing subjects such as that. I'd like you to join with me in thanking our whole panel and, particularly the main speakers.

[Applause]

NOTES ON THE TEXT

1. Norton, 1973

2. Because of her deliciously incongruous name, an oxymoron of innocence and lustiness, I had somehow pegged Satir as tall, willowy, sad-eyed, drawn, and ancient: the Virginia Woolf of mind change. Outside of sheer size — she *was* tall — nothing could have been further from the truth. The late Virginia Satir looked more like a robust and vigorous grandmother from Tarzana. During this conference, she, alone of the faculty, was available to any and all. One often came across her in corners of meeting rooms, hallway benches, the back of the press room, even in the dining area, huddled with one or two of the conference-goers, giving free advice, thoughts, ideas to all who asked. Because of her openness and availability, she was probably the most beloved of any of the faculty.

3. Ellis's convolutions with English syntax are not limited to the spoken word. In the chapter on Rational-Emotive Therapy that he composed for Corsini's *Current Psychotherapies*, he managed to come up with this whopper: *To help them change their malfunctioning, it is usually desirable to use a variety of perceptual-cognitive, emotive-evocative, and behavioristic-reeducative methods in a full therapeutic armamentarium.*

By giving him faculty status, the creators of the conference, were, perhaps, paying homage to an honorable past. In the highly repressive '50s — Ellis was one of the most outspoken advocates of an openness and freedom in sexuality and sex therapy. He and the late Alfred Kinsey probably had the most effect in opening "the dark flower" in this regards. Further, we should not gainsay a certain repetitive mordant humor in his writings: his favorite phrase for a wretched self-image in patients is called "*must*urbatory." (This phrase delights him enough to be repeated several times on the long and tortured path of the article in Corsini's book.)

4. *Wisdom, Madness, & Folly*, McGraw-Hill, 1985.

5. Pantheon, 1970.

6. Although Rogers is speaking in the first person, in the context of the interview he is in fact speaking with her voice. This is part of his technique — to shift persona every now and then, to come even closer to the client's feelings.

7. Harvard University Press, 1984.

8. Laing is speaking of the famous passage where Anna Karenina sees her husband for the first time after she has been meeting with her soon-to-be lover Vronsky: *"Oh mercy!" she says, "Why do his ears look like that?" she thought, looking at his frigid and imposing figure, and especially the ears that struck her at the moment as propping up the brim of his round hat. Catching sight of her, he came to meet her, his lips falling into their habitual sarcastic smile, and his big, tired eyes looking straight at her. An unpleasant sensation gripped at her heart when she met his obstinate and weary glance, as though she had expected to see him different. She was especially struck by the feeling of dissatisfaction with herself that she experienced on meeting him. That feeling was an intimate, familiar feeling, like a consciousness of hypocrisy, which she experienced in her relations with her husband. But hitherto she had not taken note of the feeling, now she was clearly and painfully aware of it.*

9. Indeed, two of the conference leaders died shortly after the meeting — Virginia Satir and Carl Rogers.

10. Copyright (c) 1977-1985 by the Institute for Rational-Emotive Therapy.

11. As quoted in *Samadhi: Self-Development in Zen, Swordsmanship, and Psychotherapy,* by Mike Sayama. SUNY Press, 1986.

12. From the *Reader's Encyclopedia*, William Rose Benet, Editor. Harper & Row, 1965.

13. Raymond J. Corsini, *Current Psychotherapies*. Peacock, 1984.

14. Edelwich and Brodsky in *Sexual Dilemmas for the Professional* reported statistics in 1982 of "5% - 13% of physicians and psychologists having erotic contact with their patients. More recent popular press reports give much higher figures.

15. Corsini, op. cit.

16. Corsini, op. cit.

17. Ruth Mellor had been analyzed by Otto Rank. Evidently Rank had but a few months left on a three year visa to the United States. The demands on his time were so great that he consented to work with a group of therapists in "limited therapy." This was scheduled for six months (treatments at the time took ten or twelve times as long.) Whitaker believes this might be one of the precedents for "brief therapy."

18. He was right. Sophie Freud, Margot Adler and Dieter Baumann were pictured together — along with separate photographs of Laing, Satir, and Bettelheim.

19. *The Myth of Mental Illness*, Harper & Row, 1961.

20. Obviously not. His article (which appeared ten days later) was filled with tut-tuts over the lack of consensus of the conference. He missed the stunning panoply of views offered, each with its own virtues and vices. He missed the fact that a conscientious conference-goer could pick up enough material to aid and abet, considerably, updating techniques in his or her prac-

tice. Minuchin merited two short paragraphs in the story; Szasz one; and Bettelheim and Whitaker, none.

21. Menn created "Soteria House" in Philadelphia to work with schizophrenics. The thesis was to use no medication, but rather supportive *presence*, when the patients were going through sequences of horror. It was thought that these were not unlike drug "flashbacks," and should be handled in the same way. It is reported that the best supporters for patients were people who had grown up with psychotic parents, because they had learned (in a positive way from their own childhood) that "loving and madness could coëxist." Soteria House was successful and revolutionary, but was killed by Reagan administration budget cutting.

22. One of his biographers — Jeff Zeig — contends that this might have been a seige of what we now call "post-polio syndrome" (or *Halstead's Disease*) which is characterized by fever, fatigue, intense muscle spasms, pain, and loss of muscle use. It unerringly duplicates the original symptoms of acute anterior poliomyelitus.

23. Carl Whitaker calls them "Binder & Grinder."

24. See *Advanced Techniques of Hypnosis and Therapy* by Jay Haley.